JERUSALEM MOONLIGHT

JERUSALEM MOONLIGHT

An American Zen teacher walks the
path of his ancestors

NORMAN FISCHER

Clear Glass Press
San Francisco, 1995

CLEAR GLASS PUBLICATIONS
62 Stanton Street
San Francisco, California 94114

Text excerpt pp. 70-74 from *Fodor's 1987 Israel,* ©1987 by Fodor's
Travel Publications, Inc. Reprinted by permission of the publisher.

Library of Congress Catalog Card Number: 95-067322
ISBN 0-931425-46-8

To my mother and father

Lenora Fischer (1922–1985)
Sidney Fischer (1919–1991)

who gave me more than I can ever repay

CONTENTS

PREFACE

I CONSTRUCTED this book from notes I made while I was in Israel, and from things that were happening to me at the time I was constructing it, from the spring of 1987 until the end of 1989. I revised the manuscript again in 1994.

I worked mostly in odd moments here and there in what spare time I had left over from my duties at my temple when I wasn't spending time with my family.

It's funny about writing: everything is shifting, and yet you put words down on the page and there they are. In fact you may not agree with what you wrote one week or one year later. Or even five minutes later. What actually happens — even what you think or feel — is necessarily not the same as what gets written in a book.

I've written here about family and friends and have used their names and actual incidents. I hope what I have said about everyone is kind and close to true (or at least not an out and out lie) and that you are all satisfied with the way you come out looking. My idea was to encourage the reader to feel as I do about all those portrayed here: they are good people and I am grateful to them all.

Thanks to Michael Phillips for publishing this work with the same casual and open-hearted spirit in which I tried to write it, and to Michael Wenger for giving Michael Phillips the idea.

And thanks also to my brother Jeff Fischer for, incredibly, typing the first draft of the manuscript for me from my longhand notebooks. Above and beyond the call of duty! Thanks are also due to Patricia Ikeda for Mac work, to Layla Smith for design and typesetting, and to Paul Kahn for designing the cover. And finally, thanks to the Callipeplon Society for a grant that helped with the production of this book.

"The Old City" first appeared in *Poetics Journal*; "My Mother" appeared in *Tricycle*. Thanks to Lyn Hejinian and Barrett Walter of *Poetics Journal* and Helen Tworkov of *Triycle*.

NORMAN FISCHER
Green Gulch Farm
Muir Beach, California

What are we doing, coming back here with this pain?...
What are we doing
in this dark land with its
yellow shadows that pierce the eyes?

— YEHUDA AMICHAI

What year is this he asked on the banks of the (Jordan) river.

But land is not in question here. Only the day. The range of vision.
The distance between the mountains behind the lake and the moun-
tains behind the men who face the lake.

— CARLA HARRYMAN

So I can offer nothing certain except to recount the extent of my
knowledge at the present moment. No attention should be paid to the
matter. Only to the shape I give it.

— MONTAIGNE

JERUSALEM MOONLIGHT

THICH NHAT HANH'S SMILE

REGARDLESS OF WHERE ONE IS or what occurs, the world in time resolves itself to a line of horizon edged with white cloud below a pale blue sky, in this case seen over the silver tip of an airplane's wing.

But this story begins in Watsonville several weeks ago, Watsonville, California, at a Vietnamese Buddhist monastery. I've come here with my abbot, Tenshin Anderson, and several other senior monks of the San Francisco Zen Center, to meet with Thich Nhat Hanh, the great Vietnamese Buddhist monk. Thich Nhat Hanh is in my opinion, along with the Dalai Lama, the greatest Buddhist teacher of this age. For many years in Vietnam, and then afterward in France, he pursued at once his practice of meditation and insight into the nature of reality, and his attempt to work for peace, for a humane universe, despite the fact that the political problems were insoluble. And, like the Dalai Lama, his culture broken, his world detached, exiled, witness to violence, he has had to create and master a presentation of Buddhism that speaks to present conditions, that is not an exotic product of a quiet hothouse culture of Asian bliss, but rather a clear expression of and remedy for the difficulties and joys of the present.

Thich Nhat Hanh is justly famous for his emphasis on reconciliation, his simple clear writing and speaking, his slow pace in

1

everything he does, especially walking, and his insistence on joy. "Suffering is not enough" is his point. To be aware of one's suffering and even more the suffering of others far away, but to be grateful for what is joyous presently.

He also insists that people smile. Usually people say that it's not honest to smile if they don't feel like smiling or that it is stupid to go around smiling all the time. It is too Oriental.

But Thich Nhat Hanh insists (very gently of course) that people smile and is amused by the various anti-smile arguments which seem rather beside the point to him.

When a person who has seen this much violent death tells you to smile he means it very much and in another way than we in California mean it when we tell you to smile.

Perhaps not. The political problems almost everywhere on this planet — problems which logically are within simple reach of solutions to humans since they are created exactly by humans — seem completely insoluble and the problems lead not only to a little bit of inconvenience and unhappiness but also to murder, mass death, and ultimate foreclosure of the planet on which the humans live, including perhaps all the other species that live on the planet. Perhaps the causes and effects of this disaster will prove beneficial in the long run but certainly this seems unlikely to be true in any way I or anyone else can think or write.

The trip to Watsonville takes several hours. At first we talk a lot but then we fall silent. Trees and green hills slip by. The trees made deep dramatic shadows on the hills.

None of us has ever been to this Vietnamese monastery before. We have the address but the numbers of the driveways that feed onto this narrow mountain road do not seem to make sense. We can't tell if they are increasing or decreasing. Finally it seems clear that we have passed the place. But the Abbot is sure that no, we must drive on, and exactly, though contrary to all common sense, we come to the correct number in a place where it is not supposed to be and pull into the quiet monastery.

We are greeted by a smiling young Vietnamese man with a limp, wearing brown monk's clothes, who ushers us in to speak with Thich Nhat Hanh.

The room is quiet and large with a low table in the middle of the room covered in grass mats with oriental-style pictures of squat little baseball players wielding short bats. There is a decorative Buddha standing in one corner. Thich Nhat Hanh is seated at the table. The Vietnamese abbot of this monastery offers us all tea, then smilingly and quietly withdraws.

The purpose of our meeting with Thich Nhat Hanh is to discuss with him a possible reconciliation between the Zen Center and the former abbot of the Zen Center, the American monk Zentatsu Baker. Zentatsu, aka Richard Baker, is an extraordinary man who was abbot of the Zen Center from the death of the founding Abbot Shunryu Suzuki, a wise old Japanese Zen man, in 1971, until 1983, when the disclosure of a love affair he was engaged in with a married student (Zentatsu himself is married) rocked the Zen Center, causing confusion, loss of faith, revision of expectations, and psychological disturbances among many of the members, and finally led to his forced resignation. This event, which is as yet not completely understood by anyone who was involved in it, and, like any event that happens at any time, will never be understood by anyone who was involved in it, or anyone else, was a celebrated case in the Buddhist world. Wandering Zen students reported hearing talk of it in forest monasteries in Thailand and cocktail parties among Jewish intelligentsia in the upper West Side of Manhattan Island.

Of course the confusion and grief I speak of had many complicated causes and it ran deeper than shock over a love affair involving a religious figure. People were shocked because their idea of who Zentatsu was, an idea in their own minds but also in Zentatsu's mind, was shattered. And since they had come to understand, each of us, who we were dependent on who we thought he was, we were really confused. And it raised deep questions for us about what a religious teacher actually is, a receptacle, necessarily

3

if you are going to stake your life on meditation practice, for your projections of goodness and religious aspiration and possibility. And how could such a person be an ordinary person or not an ordinary person, be enlightened or not enlightened, and what does that mean anyway. We had thought we knew. And if we didn't know, was there any such thing at all. And were we all just foolish. And could they understand about this in Japan but we couldn't understand here. And can we ever have faith in anything, trust our own hopes or anyone's hopes again. And would we have faith in our practice now in our lives or in any other person. And if we did could they stand it. Could we.

Because of all this, since 1983 relations between our former abbot and the present leadership of Zen Center have been painful.

Because of some recent overtures in the direction of peace, which have coincided with Thich Nhat Hanh's American visit, it has seemed to some members vital that today's meeting occur.

We meet for four hours of intensive and sometimes difficult discussion. Thich Nhat Hanh, talking quietly but firmly, says that in order to reconcile one side needs to take the plunge forward into the unknown territory of risk, acting with and for the dictates of its own peaceful heart, regardless of the intention of the other. Unless someone does this there can only be, since nothing remains static, a worsening or hardening of tensions.

But many of the Zen Center leaders feel that Zentatsu is wrong, power-mad, amoral, immoral, deeply unaware of and unresolved about himself, dangerous, tricky, heedless of others' needs or viewpoints, even evil.

As the discussion goes on I imagine that Thich Nhat Hanh must have made these same arguments when he was head of the Buddhist Peace Delegation to the Vietnamese Peace Talks many years ago in Paris. The arguments must have struck at that time all parties as unrealistic, laughable, or even prejudicial to each side's viewpoint, and they were not followed. The war was prolonged for many years and still in fact continues in Vietnam and among Vietnamese outside Vietnam in the form of feuds, hatreds, and animosities. I do not know whether it would have evolved differently had Thich Nhat Hanh's viewpoint been accepted. But it seems to me clear that in this case his proposals are apt.

During the discussion he talks about his own role in that distant country. He says that at one time he was advisor to an organization called School of Youth for Social Service. His function was to give a simple, practical talk once a week, and to pass out candy to the children in the villages in which the organization had its bases. He said, but when I pass out candy it is not the same as when someone else passes out candy.

How is it different from anyone passing out candy, I ask.

I will not soon if ever forget, nor do I have an interpretation for, the look on his face at that moment, nor for the gesture he made at that time with his hand and shoulders. He did not speak.

As I write I am sitting next to a young woman on the airplane. We are quite intimate together, eating, even sleeping together in a very small space but I have not spoken to her. The reason I have not spoken to her is because I want to write, and I know that if I speak to her I will learn a lot but I will be responsible to her for that knowledge and I will have to put forth much effort to be her friend. As it is I am already her friend, already her relation, but not so much as if I would speak.

Perhaps she would learn something from me but certainly not more than I would learn from her.

What would it be like to be a person from whom much could be learned but who could learn very little from others? I feel sad at this prospect. It also seems as impossibility from my present perspective.

Perhaps something like this is why we at the Zen Center had such trouble with our very talented Abbot Zentatsu Baker.

Religion is a powerful difficult aspect of the human heart, a necessary one, one that has no doubt done as much harm as good in the human past if it has not done more harm.

After our discussion with Thich Nhat Hanh we stay at the monastery for dinner — lovely Vietnamese vegetarian food. There are carrots cut in the shape of delicate swans. Many of the dishes are made of tofu, bean curd, in imitation of various kinds of meats. I had no idea tofu had so many aspects.

Darkness comes gradually as we drive home talking excitedly the whole way about our feelings about our lives and Zentatsu's life, about how to go on. We talk also to some extent about my trip to Israel, still at this time several weeks away into the future.

But at the time of this writing it is some days into the past.

I LAND

THE AIRPLANE LANDED IN ISRAEL and I got out but I did not feel anything special. I did not feel the relief gratitude sense of homecoming etc. of arrival here that I have read about in books or heard about, wanting to kiss the earth, weeping at faces seen on the street, stirred at the sound of Hebrew. People on the street seem on the whole to look like Arabs, Sephardic Jews probably, not the European Ashkenasic Jews I identify with. This ascendance of the Sephardic Jew, long the minority in Israel, is of course a much written about aspect of contemporary Israel. And Hebrew sounds like a foreign language.

But there is no question about it. These people are Jews I am a Jew.

From my earliest childhood Jewishness and the weight of meaning it bore was clear to me, and even though I resisted the chumminess of Jews, the sense of clubbiness and superiority I often sensed among the upper middle class Jews my lower middle class parents encouraged me to cultivate, I never doubted my own blood membership in the lineage, as handed down to me personally as it were from the beginnings of historical time.

I knew I was walking around in this strange and inhospitable present bearing the full weight of that baffling past.

To wander, to be outside, to struggle, to be obliged to live for reasons beyond the personal — these necessities seemed then as now clear to me, and to be the essence of my heritage.

But I do not understand the martyrdom that has held this identity together over the centuries, during the Hasmonian revolt, at Masada, in Europe during the Second World War, here in 1948. I do not understand this kind of faith if faith is what it is. Rather I feel a faith in life itself, the ongoingness of it, Jewish life or any other life. Maybe I feel about humankind in general what a Jew feels about Jews and would feel the relief in landing on the planet earth that perhaps Jews feel on landing here.

Yet undeniably I am a Jew just like all these other Jews here. It all makes perfect sense to me. Whatever Buddhist persona I may affect forget it! Right away I am in step here. I feel the same way everyone else does. I think it's wonderful that we have our own place for Jewish life. I feel perfectly at home. I could stay here forever walking down this airplane ramp into the wind, sitting in this hotel lobby, riding on this El Al airplane to Tel Aviv writing in this Israeli notebook.

And today, thinking about this in California, I am really sorry I am not in Jerusalem now. I am lonely for it as my ancestors were lonely for it for thousands of years.

Time is mixed up. The past, the present, the future...it's not all so well organized as it looks. How much time is there really between these words and the time when I was a boy at Sunday school vowing never to give God up, as the people in the story vowed, and died to their vow. Israelis are just as mixed up — Begin, Herod, Ben Gurion, King David — all mixed up in a past and present so confused there seems to be no future.

A bus takes us from the plane to the building where passports are checked at the ends of long lines. People jammed up, hot, happy, tired. Lots of Chasidic Jews wrapped in their prayerful concentration. It is nice to descend from the airplane down a metal ramp into the windy outdoors, rather than through the carpeted tube of indoor American airports.

We take another bus from Tel Aviv to Jerusalem. Tel Aviv is on the Mediterranean Sea; Jerusalem is east, in the mountains. The ride is a good look at landscape: at first coastal plains full of agricultural projects, fruit trees, grapevines, what looks like wheat, artichokes, fields of moderate size on increasingly hilly land. Gradually hills with rock shelves, hills with remnants of what must be ancient stone walls here and there. There are some trees, but they look quite young — cedars, olives, a long stretch of another reddish leafed and delicate tree I do not recognize but am greatly moved by.

So stone, rather than wood, is the characteristic building material here, a pinkish gray-brown sandstone I suppose, and the buildings, once they begin to appear on the tops of the high stony hills, are flat-roofed, uniformly colored.

There is a peacefulness to the landscape, a harshness, a profundity — one imagines how a direct relation to the Godhead would occur here, unmediated by plants and animals, the perfect place for the break-through out of shamanism into some kind of final and total sense of terrible responsibility.

Finally the square quiet stone houses on the hills increase in density, the hills increase in height number and stoniness and we are in the ancient — and new — city of Jerusalem. The first sight we glimpse on the street: young Israeli cops, two men and a woman, very swarthy, smiling, wholesome, flirting with one another. More people on the streets. They don't seem entranced by their social roles (soldiers on the streets carrying machine guns, policemen, businessmen, hotel clerks). In the way they carry themselves, speak, look around, more as who they are than the roles they inhabit. As though the function "Jew" were embedded much more deeply in them than the function "policeman," "soldier," "physician." An underlying reality or necessity much more compelling than the daily round.

This highway that connects Jerusalem to the sea has been a crucial connective artery throughout history and has therefore always been the site of heavy fighting. We see the remains of a recent manifestation of that fighting, rusted out trucks and tanks in the hills beside the road left there since the War for Independence of 1948 when this pass changed hands several times and Jerusalem almost capitulated from starvation, now left in place as war memorials, today draped with white and blue Israeli flags because it is Memorial Day. And tonight at sundown the mourning stops and the celebration of Independence Day begins.

My father and brother and I enthusiastically hit the streets: people in the streets — at first a crowd, but then hordes — bopping each other with plastic hammers that squeak when they hit you and spraying one another and us mercilessly with cans of special stuff that looks like shaving cream. Streets jammed with people of all ages — old people, kids, infants miraculously wheeled around in strollers unharmed in the jam-up of bodies, everyone happy, everyone amused, no one minds being sprayed or bopped. Up King George Street, down Jaffa Road, to Zion Square. Along the way we stop at the Great Synagogue of Jerusalem where impressive services are underway — a choir of rabbis, a cantor, a blast on the shofar.

THE OLD CITY

WE WALKED TO THE OLD CITY yesterday, the original Jerusalem on the hill surrounded now by the familiar wall built by the Crusaders. Founded by King David, destroyed rebuilt and conquered scores of times, the most contested and drastic square mile on the planet.

There must be a name for architecture in which what's outside the building is conceived of as indoor space. "City." Opposite of the California style, influenced by the Japanese, which wants to suggest the opposite: that the natural space outside extends inside. Stone buildings with narrow stone corridors between them, must be characteristic of Middle Eastern architecture: is cooler.

We toured the Moslem Quarter with a young rabbi, a native of Miami, from one of the fundamentalist Orthodox Jewish sects. It would be an education in human nature to understand the various Jewish sects with their bizarre and opposing viewpoints. Now, as throughout Jewish history, each sect is a world unto itself, suspicious of the others, convinced completely of its own rectitude.

He showed us houses in the Moslem Quarter that had formerly been Jewish houses — scars on the lintels where mezuzahs had been affixed centuries ago. Now some Jews are trying to reclaim homes in these areas. They make the claim, the rabbi tells us, that the homes were originally deeded to their families but had been seized by Christians or Arabs centuries ago during one conquest or another. So you can go to court if you have a good enough lawyer and genealogist and get the whole city back, if there were any justice at all, he explains.

After twelve centuries of this sort of plunder the city was in ruins. Not a Jew in it from then until Nachmanides returned from the Spanish inquisition in the fifth century and set up the Jewish community again miraculously (since there were no boundary indications, supposedly no maps, only rubble) in exactly the old spot.

The attitude of this young red-headed rabbi—talking excitedly, running on ahead, throwing his hands up in the air—that this street we are now walking on, with its large Herodian stones, was nothing other than the ancient suq, the marketplace, and yet the Christians make a big deal out of it and call it the Via Dolorosa, it's just a street, nothing more than an ordinary street! — that the holiness the Moslems feel for Jerusalem is not sincere, it's just a copy of what it actually is for us Jews, because presumably they're jealous of the true power of our religion — is characteristic in the power of its presentation of the cultic attitude. Something at once ecstatic and desperate about it.

The same look in the eye of the man, another American expatriate, bearded, black hat and tails, who came rushing up to us insisting we put on teffelin at the Wailing Wall: glazed, ecstatic, apocalyptic.

I think we Jews invented the cult. There is of course a strong rationalistic tradition in Judaism, begun during the time of the Rabbis in the second century, but it is there precisely as a reaction against cultism. Read Josephus' eyewitness account of the fall of the Second Temple in A.D. 70 sometime for an account of the Jewish cults around the time of Christ, whose own cult, of course, developed a not inconsiderable head of steam.

And it is impossible to deny that there is palpably afoot here throughout the city, and most powerfully of course at the holy sites and among the holy people, a definite spirit let us say beyond life, beyond the ordinary, beyond money and flesh, so that it is not surprising that someone would find it logical to throw away ordinary ways of being and be now rather in a transfigured way. And any notion that this transfiguration is not a concrete reality can be dismissed summarily, not even as a threat but as a mere joke. This attitude does not make so much sense in Cincinnati. But here in Jerusalem it is quite compelling.

The Wailing Wall built by Herod in the late Second Temple days still stands of course as the ultimate physical manifestation of this spirit, its cracks stuffed full of little pieces of paper scrawled with the prayers offered by pilgrims. And I add my own, prayerful to write in the language one breathes and dreams in automatically words of hope, making so clear the sense that the writing and speaking of words are always acts of prayer.

I roll up the little piece of paper, piece of my heart and spirit, touch the wall, put my head against the smooth stones that are cold despite the great heat of the day, close my eyes, begin to wonder where I am and who I am, think of my family and of generations and generations of people who have gone before me, and start to weep in a way that feels releasing and very natural.

Meanwhile behind me and the hundreds of other worshipers at the wall in the beautiful open courtyard, tables are set out and the Torah is being chanted in the wailing traditional way by old Sephardi men in native dress, a clutch of people around them, holding up their hands to touch the air around the scroll as it is lifted and moved about.

These words of the Torah that include universes, tell absolutely the truth, that outlast life and death.

Suddenly commotion: soldiers clear the area: someone left a bag, no one knows what it is, this is suspicious, it might be a bomb!

Apparently this sort of thing is quite normal here since this is the ideal spot on earth to leave a bomb if you are a Palestinian

13

terrorist. To prevent this there are of course serious security checks at entry points by uniformed members of Israeli Defense Forces toting machine guns. But it's not foolproof.

Soldiers in fact stand guard everywhere in the Old City. Everywhere carrying their machine guns, even on crowded streets during the Independence Day celebration May 2. But unlike the feeling in the USA where soldiers can seem affected by some Rambo-like dream of insurmountable violence and male power, and because they seldom appear on civilian streets seem nervous and out of place, almost monk-like, when they do, here the soldiers seem quite wholesome and ordinary young men and women, quite friendly and open with the populace, like boy scouts and girl scouts, except of course for the machine guns, which are also by law routinely carried by schoolteachers when they go on field trips with their students.

A country in which, hard to imagine, people in fact share a common purpose, a common life, and provide for the common defense.

We are in an enclosed vaulted area that abuts the Wall. Above us, in ancient times, was a land bridge, a huge ramp that led up to the Temple Mount. The Wailing Wall is the western retaining wall of this Temple Mount, which was a huge high flat area, about 40 acres, originally created by Solomon, in fact a kind of man made mountain, the largest such thing the world had ever seen, in the center of which was the temple.

Today the Temple Mount is controlled by the Waqf, the Muslim Supreme Religious Council, and is the site of two important mosques, the great holy sixth century Dome of the Rock, and the El Aqsa Mosque. The Dome of the Rock, one of the three holiest Muslim sites, enshrines the rock from the top of which Mohammed jumped off into heaven. It also may be the top of Mt. Moriah, where Abraham almost sacrificed Isaac.

Orthodox Jews therefore when they pray facing the Wall as they do daily in great numbers especially on the Sabbath pray facing these mosques.

Looking down through the grating I can see seventeen huge stones one below the next to the bottom layer, which is the top of the wall built on top of the original wall by King Hezikiah. Here in the Old City things are built layer by layer, the city destroyed, burned, and rebuilt on the ashes over and over again. The hills the city is built on were once much higher mountains, their comparative height reduced by all the fill in the valleys used over the centuries to build atop what had been built before.

Since 1967 when Israel recaptured the Old City there has been tremendous reclamation excavation and construction. The wide courtyard around the wall had been full of small Arab dwellings which were pulled down within three days of its capture. The spiritual surge that must have accompanied the capture of the wall after twenty centuries and twenty recent years of fighting must have been stupendous. That these had been the homes of actual people must have seemed at the time a detail hardly worth mentioning. Today the entire Jewish quarter, completely destroyed after the 1948 War for Independence during which the Arabs retained control of the Old City, has been rebuilt as a cultural and educational center. All over the city tremendous archeological digs continue layer after layer.

Up many narrow stone steps to a small yeshiva where Orthodox Kohanim (members of the ancient high priest caste) sit around tables studying. The small room feels like eighteenth century Poland, many young men, dressed in the style of that time and place, sitting opposite each other at small tables, engaged in loud disputations in Hebrew, din of voices, bodies swaying back and forth a seeming chaos of conversation. (There are in fact, I am told somewhere, more young men presently studying along the ancient rabbinical course of study here in Israel than were destroyed by Hitler). The idea is that when the temple is eventually rebuilt, which the Orthodox sects believe it surely will be, spontaneously and by Godly not human hands, the existence of the Dome of the Rock a mere detail hardly worth mentioning, the ancient rites, which have not been performed since the year A.D. 70, will once again be performed. Therefore the Kohanim, who are uniquely charged with the performance of the rites, had better bone up on them so that they are ready when the day comes: the purpose of this particular yeshiva.

And the yeshiva, as if to anticipate this new order, is located near the Temple Mount in the Moslem quarter, and has therefore been the scene of terrorism.

One can see in the eyes of Moslems the resentment of the arrogance of these Jews who clearly do not acknowledge any shred of merit in the Moslem way of life and who see right through the faces of these Moslem people into the coming millennium during which all of this city is inhabited by Jews. (As if in some supra-physical Godly manipulation of the mechanisms of time all effects between the year A.D. 70 and the millennial year are totally wiped away).

The extent to which this millennial idea, which posits a time in which history stops and all that remains is the transfiguration, conditions the root of Jewish thought is not to be underestimated.

At this point ordinary thinking itself can come to a halt. All physical and social laws are suspended. We can't even begin to think about it one way or another because our mind can't grasp it, our imaginations can't encompass it, our logic can't penetrate it. Language itself will be a completely different thing at that time.

So whatever objections we may have to such an idea now will be voided nullified and rendered absurd from the standpoint of the millennium itself.

One of the bearded black-hatted men explains to me that the way the temple will be rebuilt (this is the last historical act that announces the advent) is quite simple, it has nothing to do with the politics of the Middle East: the skies will open, the Dome of the Rock will vanish, and the temple will be lowered down onto the spot.

What about animal sacrifices, I ask him, will you do animal sacrifices again? It's not like you think of it, he assures me. It's not anything like the animal sacrifices of primitive peoples. At that time everything will be different, holy, all the rules will be changed, we can't conceive of it now.

All of this seems to me about as possible as anything else. The question of how I am going to act based on the information available to me is another question. If I can believe that the temple will be built again in this fashion can I also believe it is in fact already built only we haven't been able to notice it as yet?

A WALK ON LONG
ISLAND

Now I AM SITTING ON AN AIRPLANE that is taking me to California from New York. It is the middle of the night. The plane is dark except for a few pools of light here and there. I remember walking through the woods on Long Island with my cousin Brenda yesterday. It was lovely to see the early Spring vegetation, the new leaves pushing out on the trees, tender, light green, very fresh and startling to me. Spring does not look like this along the Coast in California. Walking along a choked woodland path near Brenda's large house — young trees, some pines, some oaks, birches, a lot of wild cherry in bloom, dogwood, many of these entwined with the honeysuckle that climbs all over eventually destroying most of it. There are some wild apple trees too in places. Everything is in bloom. Mountain laurel. I am immediately moved by these plants which remind me of my childhood, this sense of spring that I have not felt for many years.

We passed into some open meadows sparsely populated with birches and wild strawberries — the earth was uneven as in furrows, this must have been a farm not long ago — there are patches of daffodils popping up here and there, probably where the farm house was. Probably because of the low prices of crops, the difficulty and relentlessness of farm work, and the high price of suburban land, it was impossible for the farmer, elderly, his children uninterested in inheriting this place and job, not to sell the land, and now most of it, this strip temporarily excepted, holds houses of the people who drive to the city daily for work.

Land. People imagine they can buy it or sell it. Actually people do not possess land, land possesses people. Farmers know this. Do the Israelis know it? Deeds, boundaries, history, national agreements, pale in Israel, make no sense at all. Whose land any land is is a senseless question. Land is a human cry for permanence. Even if you blow it up or excavate it fifty feet down it is still there, it goes on. Yet from one moment, one second, to the next it is never the same.

A long time ago, before history, people knew about that. They had no idea about "land," and certainly no idea about "ownership." They wandered around and found things to eat and places to be. They belonged nowhere and everywhere.

As we walk Brenda is talking to me about her life. She is married to Marvin, her second husband, who is a lawyer, and they always have a very complicated life and relationship. Marvin grew up in Brooklyn, a very intelligent man who approaches the world through his intelligence; Brenda, also quite intelligent, is powerfully emotional and her emotions are masked often to herself. Since Marvin had two children by a previous marriage and since Brenda also had two children by a previous marriage and since all these children intersect their marriage each with his and her own complex need and emotion there is no end to the trouble and confusion they can all experience. All of this we discuss as we walk along the woodland path.

A MEAL WITH SHLOMO

WE'RE IN BRENDA AND MARVIN'S large colonial style house eating dinner. It's twilight, a beautiful light. Brenda and Marvin, Karen, Brenda's daughter, and Shlomo, Karen's boyfriend, and me. Everyone is giving me good advice about my trip, which begins tomorrow, to Israel. They have all been there: Marvin has a daughter who lives at Kibbutz Ma'aleh Hamishma and he's been there several times with Brenda; Shlomo has lived most of his life in Israel; Karen lived there for a few years in college. She and Shlomo met there.

Shlomo is a Yemmenite Jew who has "come down" (this is the phrase, it is the opposite of Aliah, to "go up," to immigrate to Israel) from Israel to the States to stay for an indefinite period. He's a lively person, loud and assertive, straightforward, humorous, possessive of a certainty and lack of self consciousness typical of Middle Eastern Jews. It is I think an almost intentional personal quality, a positive revolt against the image of the Jew as timid and thoughtful.

Shlomo on the other hand is also not naive. As an Arab Jew he knows he can't be accepted into this upper middle class American Jewish situation, and the unspoken obviousness of this to all present creates an atmosphere.

It is a difficult situation for all young Israelis — to want out of what is clearly an impossible situation at home, but into what? And how escape the imperative to support the nation which is after all not only a nation but the answer to centuries of spilled Jewish blood.

And worse still for someone like Shlomo who is heir to a strong traditional way of life. To get out from under the weight of that tradition, to exchange it for total freedom in the modern world: total freedom without any meaning. Shlomo works as a carpenter. He's done this for a few years. He tells his mother and brother in Jerusalem he'll be back, when he doesn't know, he tells himself he'll be back, he has no plans one way or the other. They all say, as Jews have said for centuries, "Next year."

CRAZY

THIS UPI ARTICLE appeared in the *San Francisco Chronicle* on March 26, 1987:

BIZARRE MANIA AFFLICTS TOURISTS WHO VISIT THE HOLY LAND
by David Mould
Jerusalem — Psychologists in Jerusalem are studying a rare and puzzling disorder that transforms seemingly normal people into lunatics after touring the Holy Land.

"Most of the victims are Protestants from the United States," said Dr. Carlos Bar-El, Israel's district psychologist for Jerusalem and an expert on the condition.

Bar-El said that after about three days of visiting holy sites such as Christ's tomb or the Garden of Gethsemane, "something very, very strange suddenly comes over them.

"They don't eat. They don't drink. They don't sleep. They become manically psychotic. We really don't know what causes it, but it only happens to about 15 or so people a year and it only happens in Jerusalem — nowhere else in the world."

Bar-El, director of a clinic that treats the condition, wrote his first research paper on the subject three years ago. He said there were various theories on what caused it but said they were all too new to discuss.

"It afflicts people who are otherwise perfectly normal," Bar-El said. "The one thing they all seem to have in common is that they are deeply religious."

One American woman, an elementary school teacher, was brought to Bar-El's Kfar Shaul hospital when she bolted naked from her hotel room after a two-hour hymn-singing spree.

"She locked herself in (the hotel room) for two hours and she sang and sang in a very peculiar voice," Bar-El said. "She said she wanted to be in the street without clothes and made an attempt to get away from the hotel nude."

Another U.S. patient was a 40-year-old college professor who came to Israel to conduct Biblical research.

Almost all of the victims recover in about a week; afterward, most offer strikingly similar descriptions of their feelings.

"They say it comes over them very quickly and hits them very hard," he said. "They say they feel somehow different. They feel excitation and get an urge to make some kind of change in the world..."

PRAYING AND WRITING

Now I'm sitting in the lobby of the Windmill Hotel in Jerusalem sipping decaf coffee, watching "The Thorn Birds" on TV, and listening to a lively conversation in an unidentifiable foreign language, not Hebrew, among people sitting in a grouping of chairs nearby.

I'm not interested in recording what occurs. Not at any time but particularly not now traveling with my father and brother and not wanting to inconvenience their schedules by insisting on time to write in these notebooks. Usually I don't keep diaries or journals. I do have very many notebooks full of various kinds of writing, mostly poetry and other kinds of unclassifiable writing I and other people seem to agree to call poetry. I used to try to write prose but that ended with my involvement, for many years, with Zen meditation. I found my experience was getting very slow and deep and impossible to describe; I found it no longer possible or desirable to divide life up into the time of life and the time of writing about the time of life; and in any case the writing was never describing the life. And I could not keep on doing it that way so I had to find other ways of doing it and I found ways that pleased me and said what needed to be said. I was lucky to find other writers of my generation in the same dilemma I was in and together we made a way of writing that pleased us and said what needed to be said, and many of my friends wrote about how we did this, wrote literary theory and criticism, started magazines and institutions, and some even got degrees and took over English departments in important universities. The enemies of what we wrote thought it didn't make any sense, didn't express normal human feeling, the stuff that poetry had always been about. But I think it expressed all that but expressed it just a bit more honestly and accurately, taking into account the fact that words have their own lives too and that the people that we are cannot so simply be defined.

I find a peacefulness in the aloneness of writing now, it is its own validation, apart from communication, it is in this sense holy, the speaking, the setting down of words, itself a kind of redemption, if I can use these words here in Jerusalem, it is the humanness of us, our curse and at the same time our blessing. We describe the world to ourselves, inevitably, in the words we use to talk to ourselves and others; to make that description is what it means to praise God, which we must do, and in the doing of it we inevitably become confused, and knowing that we have to have religion, to try to work our way out of it.

This is all very good to think about but it feels very different tonight, here in Efrat, the West Bank settlement for young families twenty-five minutes by car from Jerusalem, where I attend synagogue with about forty men. The no-nonsense schoolroom where we pray is crowded with purposeful young fathers, lots of devotion and fervor but not fanaticism, these are lawyers, doctors, policemen, administrators, modern orthodox Jews, cheerful and tough, full of faith, and there is a great sense of life's affirmation, of community, in their melodic speeches to God.

NAMES

Today is a day with the Israeli Fischers. They met us early this morning at the Windmill Hotel. Simon and Hilda Fischer, my father's first cousin and his wife. Simon is a quiet philosophical man, very religious in the modern Orthodox persuasion, small round man with a beautiful white-bearded face and constant half-smile; Hilda plump, talkative, anxious, charging around here and there, needing every situation to be totally under control. We drive around the city in traffic in the heat trying to find the Herzl monument — first one way then another way, back and forth, zipping through traffic, sighing and starting over, cursing and turning around again, finally getting to the site on a high hill and wandering around again among the pine trees of the military installation looking for the tomb — getting directions from the military personnel, being on the wrong side of a barbed wire fence, unable to enter, going back, Hilda talking a mile a minute about the virtues of Israel, her children, her past, her house, the settlement where they live, etc. Finally, and purely by chance, we do stumble onto the tomb of Herzl — his father and mother are interred nearby; it seems to be what the government does for heroes — buries them under a modest monument then searches the world over for their parents' bones to bring them there too to rest in perpetuity in the holy ground there beside them — one of the many unimaginable things the government routinely does here — acting more like an extended family than a government — such as passing a law that every school in the country has to have an armed guard on duty every day forever since once many years ago twenty-five children were killed in a terrorist attack. Near the tomb there's a large public arena where large scale national events are held — the bleachers for yesterday's Independence Day celebrations are being taken down today by soldiers as we wander around through the public space asking them for directions to our car which we parked somewhere we forget exactly where, Hilda yelling at Simon who shrugs his shoulders and takes off in another direction.

From there we go back into the fierce traffic, scooting around, zipping up and down, finally arriving at Yad Vashem, the Holocaust Memorial, which is a big open barn-like building made of rough stones, very simple, with a platform inside overlooking a large railed-in area completely empty except for names inscribed in the floor in Hebrew and Roman characters, the names of each of the concentration camps used by the Nazis during the War. And a flame continuously burning at the end of the room in some kind of violently twisted iron vessel.

The names. I had the impulse to pull out my notebook and very simply write down these names but it (notebook) was locked up in the trunk of Simon's car. There is something very eloquent in this simple inscription of just the names. As here in Israel the names of places people will live and die for — Jerusalem, Hebron, Judea, Sumaria.

Is the name connected to a particular place or person or is the name rather not a series of symbols, signs, that make a light in the human mind, around which many emotions thoughts and impressions cluster? Am I my name am I something else or is someone else my name? Where are the places or the people connected to these names exactly?

I have a strong sense of history and of time's passage walking down the path in the Martyr's Forest that leads us out of Yad Vashem, lined with trees planted for and dedicated to individual non-Jews who helped save Jewish lives from Hitler's grip, talking with Hilda about her family of several generations, the sense of the names, the past, almost independent of the people who bore them, the actual experiences, but the names which shape events, named events, and the names of course go on. It is very strange to imagine: all of this actually happened. Memorials like this are to make sure no one ever forgets it.

Then a bird sang, some kind of bird I've never seen and don't know the name of, the whistle of the bird brings me up to the present, just the hearing of it, and beyond the present, onto an expanse of time, in which names float and dissolve like clouds in the sky.

Judaism is a religion of names. We receive our names from generations previous and it is for our names that we work hard all our lives pouring our hearts into our names, which we pass onto our children, our most cherished heritage. I think there are many passages in the bible and other Jewish wisdom books referring to the value of a good name, greater than riches etc.

It must be because of names and emphasis on names (they almost become gods in themselves, transcending the daily life) that the murder of so many Jews during the Second World War blazes so in history. Because of the names and the strong adherence to names over the centuries on the part of the people. God's name, the mysterious name, hardly ever uttered but constantly referred to. And so because of this we are separate, the people of the name, and because separate, and, we need to face this, perhaps aggressively separate, we are persecuted, not only by Hitler but for millennia before, our shining name also serving as a symbol for the "them" it separates us from and it enrages them.

Of course many other peoples have been decimated, have disappeared entirely, during the course of human history. Gary Snyder told me yesterday, as we were walking on the University of California at Davis campus, which had been in fact a sizable Indian village at one time, that the native population of the Americas at its height was somewhere in the neighborhood of twenty million souls. But they couldn't write and without a great deal of attention paid to the written page could not emphasize the names and did not remember and could not let everyone else know to remember.

Armenians were killed by the millions, Africans, Tibetans, Chinese, Russians, but we do not remember even these as we remember the special circumstance of the Jews' murders because of language and names.

Today at a retreat at Green Gulch Farm Zen Center someone asked the Tibetan lama Tara Rinpoche how the law of karma, of retribution, applies to the Chinese invasion of Tibet. He said that clearly the Tibetans were invaded (1.2 million killed since 1959) because of their own past evil deeds in former lives and it was up to them, the Tibetans, to use this invasion, which of course they opposed and still do vigorously oppose, to deepen their spiritual practice, to purify themselves. This does not mean, simple-mindedly, that the invasion was their own fault, that the Chinese had nothing to do with it. But it prevents too much bitterness and it promotes clearer action.

Can I think of a better way than this to deal with the outrageous persistence of human injustice and violence not only against us Jews, but rampant almost anywhere you look?

If there are evil people, independently, inherently, evil, and we have to be on the alert to watch for them, will our alertness our expectation our projection not increase their evil? Are they not evil dependent on conditions which can be addressed? And if we understand these conditions perhaps we can reduce the evil.

A human mind must be always responsible for his or her own human life. This does not mean a stupidity or a failure to analyze situations for what in them is built in to make life difficult for some and easy for others. The depth of human confusion is very great. But how else but through complete responsibility find peace, which is not quietness, but the active moving into and through, rather than around, conflict.

We ended our day at the office of Moishe Fischer, my cousin, at the Hadassah Hospital. The five of us, Simon, Hilda, my father, my brother Jeff, and me straggling along the long corridor to the door of his office. It was very strange to see the name FISCHER transliterated into Hebrew characters on a plaque on his door.

GREEN GULCH

I LIVE AT GREEN GULCH FARM Zen Center, a Zen Buddhist temple just north of the Golden Gate Bridge, on the ocean. About ten or fifteen long-time Zen practitioners live here, with about thirty or so more coming and going, staying for as short a time as three days, or as long a time as several years.

We rise early every morning and put on our robes and sit in our large meditation hall that was at one time a cattle barn.

During the day we work on the farm or in the garden or in the kitchen.

We are always thinking about what this Zen practice can be and how we can do it. A lot of people come to try it out, more and more as life gets more confusing at the end of the millennium.

For a long time we were on a kind of Japanese "trip" (as we used to use this word trip twenty years ago). We were young people fed up with 60s USA culture and we thought we could start over again and be Japanese or Zen or something else other than what our parents told us about or we saw on the TV. But after all these years we found out that we are really American Judeo-Christian people and we can't be Japanese. The more we understand Japanese people the way they actually are and ourselves the way we actually are the more we can see we can't begin to understand them.

But after more than twenty years I have put on these robes each morning more days in my adult life than I have not put them on.

So it doesn't sound right either to forget the whole thing and do something else. This thing now is what I am and I am what it is.

For a long while we had a religious idea about how Zen was supposed to be but now more and more we can see that this Buddhism is not a great idea about how things are supposed to be or how we would like to imagine them but rather it is a realistic way to go about day by day the job of finding out what is actually there in life not what we may wish is there, and, finding out gradually what is there, to be happy and to help others be happy as much as we can.

At one time the kind of talk represented by the arrangement of words in that paragraph would have sounded rather sentimental to me. I was a great fan of truth. What I liked about Zen was its kamikaze frontal assault on truth no holds barred. Happiness was not part of it.

Meditation really does help. Sometimes we sit in the meditation hall all day or for two or three days or for a week, taking all our meals in meditation, not sleeping too much. Little by little this way you can forget who you think you may be, forget the past present and future, forget your name, and just look at experience itself as it unfolds. This is very restful and in the long run it is very helpful.

The young people at Green Gulch always fought a lot in the old days. We had Zentatsu to lead us in his creative inimitable way, giving us all kinds of challenges and ways of thinking about what we were doing. But we didn't really talk to one another much about it, and since there was always so much to do, what with farming, which is very hard work, and all the demands of the formal religious practice, we had a lot of squabbles but we thought it was unzen to squabble so we just quietly went to our

rooms or sat in the meditation hall mad at one another sometimes for years at a time.

We were just like an average American family in a lot of ways.
But in the last few years without Zentatsu to inspire us we realized we had to inspire each other so we began talking to each
other and we saw that we had a lot of preconceptions about each
other and so we studied the Buddhist teachings about how to talk
to one another and how to practice kindness and generosity. All
of this made life on the whole more interesting happier and more
challenging.

We have planted a lot of trees on the surrounding hills. Some
of them are fairly tall by now.

I live with my wife and sons. It is such a brief time I have to be
with them before one of us gets old and dies or dies without
getting old that it is a precious time and even though I complain,
because I enjoy complaining, it is in my blood to complain and
argue with the universe, I am happy every day to be able to spend
this time with them.

I am also regularly surprised and impressed by the various
people who come here to practice. They are an exhaustible source
of wonder, each one different completely, each one really courageous, each one with a different slant on reality.

Every day I walk down the path from my house to the zendo
and up the path back to my house. The fruit trees the grass the
hillsides the position of the sun all are different every time I make
that walk.

Yesterday I discovered for the first time that when you walk
you can only see one foot at a time, never two feet. One foot is
always disappeared. It's amazing. Try looking some time at your
feet when you walk.

IN THE ISRAEL
DISCOUNT BANK

THE MAN WALKS QUICKLY across the room and opens a desk drawer, pulls out several forms, leaves them on the desk, walks away without closing the drawer.

Simon and my father are depositing ten thousand American dollars in the bank in a complex transaction involving Israeli banking law and the relative value of foreign currencies.

I have never been on particularly friendly terms with money or understood it particularly well. As far as I can tell, what money is is the potential to purchase something later. As a thought, it also creates self respect and power for those who have it and despair and greed for those who don't because it is an agreed upon social value that is very concrete; you either have it or not; it is not a matter of opinion.

This bank is small, a local branch. It feels more like a barber shop than a bank.

The branch manager's shirttails keep coming out, he keeps tucking them back in, his pants are too tight, his paunch is hanging over them.

Now it is all done by machine instantly and there aren't any lines.

I can get money by making something and selling it or by doing something for someone but how can anyone get money itself to make more money without the use of any other materials or physical labor? Yet this is what they do and in fact, as far as I can tell, this is the only way to get a lot of money in a short lifetime.

It is obvious to me that no one who works for a living at something is ever going to get enough money.

I myself would never work for a living: no amount of money could begin to compensate me for even a moment of my life's time which once gone will never come back again no matter how much money I may acquire to buy it back.

We walk out of the bank into Simon's car. It's early in the morning of a clear hot day. The streets of the West Bank settlement high on a hill are clean and free of traffic.

ON THE WEST BANK

I WENT AGAIN YESTERDAY with Simon and Hilda to the Hadassah Hospital to look in on Moishe. He is head of the outpatient department of the hospital. He is an intense intelligent talkative man in his late thirties, of medium height, bald head showing through sandy-colored hair under kipah, thick glasses covering very bad eyes that are generally half-closed when he speaks. He has a lot genuinely to say, to inform us as much as possible about Israel. He made Aliah about nine years ago, an immigrant, as are his parents, from the USA, and is passionate about the country.

He gives us a tour of the hospital that consists of introducing us to many people and of looking at a nuclear medicine machine that takes a picture of internal organs after you swallow a radioactive substance (manufactured in Israel! Moishe states very proudly — our prices are competitive) and another machine that measures the flow of blood through the veins with some kind of sonar device. (I want to take this test, Hilda insists. I want to see if I have a condition.)

Nearly everyone we meet in the corridors is an American expatriate. The hospital looks and feels like any modern hospital — clean, bright, efficient, not enough windows.

The hospital seems very quiet, not many people around, very well organized.

Moishe on the various Jewish sects: the modern orthodox (that's what he is) wear the little knit kipot and apparently hold rather mainstream twentieth century views about money, the state of society, politics, fashion, culture etc. The many sects of Hasidim are mainly distinguished by the various places in Europe where they originated. The Lubovitchers are powerful here. They are Zionists (unlike the Satmars — a minority, a very small minority, as he assures me, who do not believe in the state, burn the flag etc.) who have an excellent sense of PR: their main public event is a yearly dinner for children whose fathers have been killed in military service, and they are quite respected for their work. Although about sixty percent of the Jews in the country are secular, they seem to all have a strong respect for traditional Jews though at the same time they think they're a little crazy and that some are even dangerous.

We leave the hospital and are off to visit the scale model of the Old City of Jerusalem (Second Temple times) located near the Holyland Hotel. Very interesting to see the city laid out most likely as it was in the time of Herod. To see the temple and wall surrounding it, race track, theater, palaces. A mighty city. Herod wanted it that way. He was of course a Romanized Jewish king, not terribly popular with the people. The idea of a theater in the Holy City was considered a blasphemy. But the Romans had one so Herod had one.

The Romans always had a hard time understanding the Jews. Other nations could quickly see the great civilizing advantages of Roman hegemony. The Romans felt they were performing a great service by conquering and therefore civilizing the world. Why did the Jews persist in their folly? They were the most troublesome of subjects. Even Herod, one of their own (most other nations in the fold were ruled by Roman governors), could not contain their hysterical will for independent worship. What was so important, so blasted special, about this nameless god they insisted on against all reason and self-advantage?

Then through Bethlehem where we visited the tomb of Rachel, Jacob's wife of the Bible — in a very modest rundown building on a major thoroughfare — guarded by soldiers on ground level on this side and above on rooftops on that side of the street — consists of a pillar or mound of some kind covered by a blue cloth — people touch this mound and pray — Rachel is woman, mother, wife — men pray on one side, women on the other — one fellow in a black hat, beard and coat, though it is a hot day, breaks into sudden sobs as he prays — Dad and I, thinking of mother, pretty glum—then back into the car with Simon and Hilda, car stalls, bucks, lurches (Don't worry, Hilda says, it's gonna start, have a candy, here come on, take one, take two — as Simon hopelessly hits the steering wheel, clucks his lips, repeats as he has several times this day, I don't know what's wrong with it. I had the mechanic check it — he cleans the carburetor, adds a new part, takes out a part, it's fine for a week, now again it's the same thing, I paid lots of money for this car) and off to Efrat, the West Bank settlement where Moishe and Panina live with their two children.

We pass the Arab refugee camps which now have a high fence around them because they throw stones at the Israeli soldiers across the street.

The Palestinian refugees of the West Bank are certainly the victims of the political confusion here that has lasted these forty years. The UN proposed a partition of the Holy Land in 1947, part of the territory to go to the Palestinian people, part to the Jews. It was an attempt to get the best out of a bad situation: the British had promised everything to everyone to achieve their own interests; the Palestinians and Jews had lived together in the same cities for centuries, pretty complicated to carve out a territorial solution: the attempt was unsatisfactory. The Jews would have been forced to accept it (their situation in 1947 was weak) but the Arab leaders, in a fit of pique, and including the Palestinian Mufti, an hysterical Fascist madman who received this lifetime religious-temporal post through a colossal screw-up by the British, rejected the partition plan. This meant war. When the Israeli rag-tag army went on the march in the Galilee the Palestinian citizens, who were the majority there, fled — they were convinced, and not without at least one dramatic piece of evidence, an act of terrorism committed by the Stern gang, that they would be massacred if they did not. None of the Arab states did much for them. It seemed very satisfactory to let them fester as a goad against Israel, and they have festered since. To be sure, Ben-Gurion was not a humanitarian interested in fair-minded compromise. He wanted Jewish turf and was ruthless and tricky in the getting of it. He was in fact about as good at geopolitical and grassroots political manipulation as King David or any other nation-creating leader has ever been. But it took a lot of cooperation to create this mess.

The fact is the Arab leaders of 1947 were by and large fairly mixed up people who were not yet ready to do justice to the possibilities of the twentieth century. A pity they could not have seen the establishment of a sophisticated European-style state in their midst as a benefit. In fact it could have been, still could be, of great benefit to them.

But this is a wonderful dream, my dream. Waking up you hear the sounds of the stones the Palestinian kids are throwing at the Israeli Defense Forces soldiers, the sounds of the flames of the cars that are burning with their Molotov cocktails, and, far worse than this, you are hearing on the radio and reading in the papers of the brutality of those IDF forces, frustrated, angry, at the ends of their ropes, caught between the brutality of the past, and the fear of brutality in the future, in a brutality of the present in which they throw people off roofs and beat people in jails after dragging them out of their homes.

We drive through hilly rocky country. Not golden hills as in California or rugged rocky peaks like Colorado but wide broad gently rising slopes, green, and uniformly scattered with boulders.

All Jerusalem is constructed of this pinkish "Jerusalem stone" (an ordinance says so), the architecture square and massive, interconnecting courtyards and corridors...

And rising up here in the midst of the hills, at the top of one of them, is a settlement made of this stone, houses of a great variety of shapes, although of a general uniform appearance, over-looking valleys all around, crisp clean air, lots of wind — Effrat, a town of Biblical times in this spot now reconstructed five or so years ago, one of the infamous West Bank settlements. About two hundred families live here (in Israel, population is measured in families, not individuals) with new construction going on every-where (designed by Jews, built by non-citizen Arabs).

A young American-born rabbi presides over the congregation in Effrat — many of his followers from Manhattan (he had one thousand families in the Lincoln Center synagogue) have fol-lowed him here. The settlement consists of, in addition to Ameri-can immigrants, also South Africans, Israelis, a Mexican family — about ninety percent Orthodox although it is not a closed com-munity. He's managed to build in just a few years a residential high school, an elementary and middle school — huge new complex on the next hill. Most of the families here have young children. The children are everywhere in the streets riding toy cars, trikes, boys wearing kipot, an average of four to a family.

The buildings are designed like an intricate block structure on the hillside with connecting courtyards, terraces, like the rebuilt Jewish quarter in Jerusalem.

Moishe and Panina have a small house with a tiny back yard, a half wall between it and the neighbor's tiny yard, and from that you can look up and see the stone walkway connecting the various other buildings — a very familiar communal architectural arrangement, which assumes everyone knows everyone else's business and they do.

Kids are constantly farmed out here and there — they walk from the age of two to the day care center just a few meters away where they stay all day 7:30 A.M. to 4 P.M. with people who take care of them with great dedication — as a career, Moishe explains.

His kids — in a chaos in the small house in which they, three of the four of them, sleep in the same room, yelling, fighting, running in and out, climbing up on the air ducts to the air raid bunker below which by law must be included in settlements of this sort — all speak English as well as Hebrew, TV is often in English, soldiers on the street speak perfect English, everyone in this world seems to speak perfect English.

The kids are really good, Panina tells me over dinner, as Chana crawls under the table looking for pieces to the new plastic bracelet Hilda just got her that fell off, and Ari stalks off and slams the door upstairs because Moishe turns off the TV and the little girl yells and slinks down off her chair because she doesn't like the food — it's sharp, she says in Hebrew, and I don't know where Nathaniel is, the infant boy, but he does his share of yelling too — and the odd thing is that yes, they do seem on the whole to be quite good kids, well behaved, and it is remarkable how Panina and Moishe are able to manage complicated discussion of Israeli economics and sociology while they eat and jump up and down with the children but they do.

Cars in Israel are heavily taxed — Volvos cost fifty thousand dollars — yet people have them! Although salaries in Israel are about a fourth of what they are in the states, Moishe and Panina bought a small apartment in Jerusalem some years ago and were able to sell it at a high profit to build here, because, I suppose, of inflation, which Peres was able to hold down mainly by devaluing the shekel, one thousand to one. Before that salaries were so high the pay vouchers did not have enough room to write down all the digits — people made millions a month — and as soon as they were paid spent it all. Now things are more stable.

We attended Mincha — it's an average day, a Monday or Tuesday, and forty to fifty men show up to pray. Even Fred (from Alabama) who is head of security — he wears a pistol — as do people now and again. It is not unusual. Here everyone participates in the defense of the community, there is a rotation, patrolling all night, the computerized lists are posted on the wall in the synagogue.

IDOLATRY

ARCHEOLOGISTS AT QUMRAN found Roman pottery that had been captured by the Jews during the Roman Wars. The Jews had defaced the images that decorated the pots.

The ancient Jewish prohibition against images applies equally to writing: representation of life in any artistic form is strictly prohibited. So there is only one theme art can deal with: the Absolute. To get stuck in life, to be caught in the net of the forms of life, not to see beyond them to the source, is idolatrous. It had to be. To plunge passionately into relationship with the Absolute has been the struggle, the struggle against our own human nature, for Jews from the beginning.

"The tendency of the Jewish writers to see everything from the standpoint of God: lacking our Western historical sense, they mix up past present and future and refer to contemporary persons under the names of legendary figures," Edmund Wilson wrote in his book *The Dead Sea Scrolls,* by way of explaining why it is difficult to tell who is who or what period we are in in the earliest Jewish historical writings.

And the idea is to live deeply, in and for God, dedicated completely to Him, seeing through the particularity of the net of this life into a broader Life that is His Life. Hence the very complicated Jewish codes that tell us how to do everything: how to wash our hands, what fabrics to wear and not to wear, what combinations of food to eat and not to eat, how to kill our meat, nip off the ends of our penises, dedicatory words to say when we do this and that and so on. To make sure we don't forget. To live in time but not be bound by time. To admit, at every turn in a life that must be lived in time, the Timeless.

You and I come and go. But the community, fused together by these ways of remembering, persists, a kind of permanent always changing organism, a being whose essence is an extended conversation with God over the millennia.

It isn't that you shouldn't represent life in art; rather it's not possible to do so. There's a story about the literary apprenticeship of Guy de Maupassant under the tutelage of Flaubert. The story goes that once they went for a walk and after the walk Flaubert said to de Maupassant, did you notice that concierge down the block? Your skill should be such that you could portray her in such a way that anyone taking that walk later would easily recognize her. But I would say, you should be able to portray her so precisely, with such depth of vision, that no one, not even she herself, would be able to recognize her.

Things are slipping away even as I am writing these sentences. The situation in Israel when I visited there in 1987, just before the start of the Intifada, is not what it is now, after the ending of the Intifada and the beginning of a long but hopeful, and at one time inconceivable, peace plan, and it is not what it is when you read these words. By now I have almost completely forgotten about that trip and the world has changed three times over since that day I walked the streets of Effrat with my relatives. But still I go on this way talking and trying to understand.

I think Buddha had a similar teaching about idolatry: don't make things into signs, images, and concepts. Of course you do that. But don't get caught by that, don't act on that too much.

One more story, this one about a Catholic monastic.

As part of his mystical training (and this is a true, twentieth century story) his teacher told him to climb to the top of a mountain, take a look at the view, and come back and tell him what he saw. Now this monastic was not a robust man and the trail only went part way up the mountain. There was much brush to cut through, and confusion over lack of a clear way, and higher and higher he fought his way. Finally, exhausted, discouraged, almost at dark, he came to the top, into the clearing, and could look all around and in a rush of comprehension it did come to him: there is no such thing as God.

JERUSALEM AGAIN

I WOKE UP THIS MORNING feeling as if someone had hit me over the head. I slipped out of the room where Dad and Jeff, my brother, still slept, to write this in the "Montefiore Room," the hotel dining room. Every morning there is a buffet table here full of all possible breakfast fare: fish, eggs, toast, yogurt, fruit, fresh and pickled vegetables, cereal hot and cold, milk, coffee, juices, rolls, as much as you can eat. I keep eating too much of it. I like to eat only a little but when there is a lot of food around I eat it.

Someone just dropped the top of the aluminum hotel pan that keeps the eggs warm — crash! Last night the waiters in the restaurant kept breaking glasses and dishes — smash!

The guests of the hotel all look like they need exercise.

Everywhere in Israel you see soldiers — always young people who look on the whole rather cheerful carrying machine guns, wearing boots, clean green fatigues.

Everyone joins the army after high school for four years before college, so there is the feeling of the army as a kind of college or pre-college, a peer group experience for people eighteen to twenty-one.

In the Old City yesterday we saw a large contingent of soldiers walking around with a guided military tour. Many of the soldiers were young women wearing makeup, jewelry, and contemporary hair styles. Their uniforms were somehow fitted to look very attractive and nearly stylish. They looked more like sorority sisters than soldiers, flirting, joking; strangely, many of them spoke English without any accent, was it a brigade of Americans in the army for summer vacation? Walking through a narrow street I want to pass by three soldiers, to walk between them but I can't do it without butting up against their three machine gun barrels — I decide to go around. I am very conscious of the machine guns as lethal weapons that might by mistake go off but the soldiers don't seem particularly to be worried about this.

Youth is a good time for soldiery and bravery. It is the age of romance and love and death. Probably throughout history a few old men interested in power and wealth led many young men interested in glory to the slaughter: what war is, or was. Now it may be nothing at all, and this is the problem with it.

People tell me the Israeli soldiers are not particularly in love with their army obligation but neither do they appear to be suffering too much nor to have assumed new and absurd identities by virtue of their uniforms.

Soldiers in Jerusalem seem to provide security in areas where you'd expect the police. This is because they are empowered to guard the national border, and in Jerusalem the border is nearly everywhere.

The numbers '48 and '67 are constant references here — this was destroyed in '48, this was in Arab hands before '67 etc. The national boundaries of Israel have been in constant dispute from the beginning, and have always been arbitrary. They were hardly spoken of in '47 before they were changed after the war of '48 and changed again in '67 and '73 and with the Egyptian settlement at Camp David in '79. It is easy to see why for Israelis the Bible is as real a fixed point in determining boundaries as any other. To the rest of the world, at least until the collapse of Communism, national boundaries seemed almost eternal and the politics of the last century constituted the only reality; here, the tremendous archeological work constantly going on, more of which begins after each war when new territory is taken, makes Biblical time much more of a living reality that one can imagine outside of Israel, particularly here in the United States, where what is old is a '57 Chevy, and it is no surprise then that some of the greatest Israeli military men (Dayan, Yadin) have also been archeologists.

Military strategy and prowess — tactics of surprise and daring to defeat much larger armies — and using clever politics to play off power against power in a situation in which large empires push their own interests on strategic foreign soil — this you can read about in the Bible, in histories of the Jewish people, in the excavation reports of the present — as well as in the daily Israeli newspapers.

A friend gave me a thick book on Israel by Noam Chomsky. I read the whole thing not without a little grief. Chomsky documents in a totally convincing way the fact that the Israelis, with their overlay of European socialist rhetoric, do not in fact play by the rules they espouse and are constantly manipulating a stupid and unsuspecting Western public into seeing them as courageous outnumbered victims when in fact they are more like ruthless territory-grabbing aggressors. Chomsky's facts I'm afraid are airtight but also I believe he misses the main point and I think is touchingly naive in this. It is certainly true that the Israelis do not play by the rules but they never have and never intended to. Cleverness double-speak and manipulation rationalized by national survival against great odds and played out against the background of a population quite sincere in its agony of high moral questioning, background and foreground almost always in opposition and yet mutually supportive, has been and is the strategy. It is a very sophisticated situation. The interpenetration, for good and ill, of religion and politics.

In Israel the army is not a political option, it is as concrete, as close, as getting out of bed in the morning or washing the dishes at night.

INSURANCE

I'M SITTING IN MY SEAT IN THE AIRPLANE writing longhand in this Israeli notebook, trying to work out really some way to understand what has always been happening to me since the beginning. There are white clouds over the edge of the wing.

It has always been a big problem for Jewish commentators on the Bible: why is it that the first letter of the first word of the Bible bereshit ("in the beginning") begins with a bet, the second letter of the alphabet, and not with an aleph, the first letter (why we call it "alphabet," and not "betaalph"). Clearly there must be some explanation for this.

The reason why is because of the form of the letter bet, a square with the left side removed. It means that, first of all, because it is not the first letter there is really no beginning even though it says "in the beginning." So we can never trust our language to say exactly what is going on, especially when it talks about time, which it always talks about when it talks about what is, which is in time, and includes everything language talks about. So language is a trick. It looks like it makes sense to us but really it doesn't.

Second, according to the shape of the letter bet we can see that creation or existence keeps closed to us what is above, what is below, and what is behind. The only thing open is what is right in front of us (the left side of the square, since Hebrew runs right to left).

This is why in order to write realistically, really realistically, I have to stay in my seat on the plane. Later on I can type all this. I'm not kidding you.

I got to talking with the woman sitting next to me. She's Chinese, lives in Vancouver, British Columbia (I'm en route to Vancouver to lead a Zen retreat), but used to live near San Francisco. She sells insurance and when I express a serious interest in life insurance, something which I am very interested in although I know almost nothing about it, she takes a great interest in me.

We discuss at length various options I might exercise in order to "protect" (meaning "get money to") my family in the event of my death, which she reminds me although I already know, is certain. She gives me her card. I am looking for the card now among the various business cards on my desk but I can't find it.

When I indicate that actually I'm not going to buy any insurance just yet she suddenly loses interest in the conversation and goes back to reading her magazine. I go back to writing this.

The pilot says it's going to be raining in Vancouver.

ISAMU NOGUCHI

THE ISRAEL MUSEUM IS IN THE NEW PART of Jerusalem, near the Knesset. It's a big modern building, outside it and to the rear is the Billy Rose Sculpture Garden designed by Isamu Noguchi, beautiful sweeping curved terraces, pebbled and white, full of carefully placed sculptural objects, at the edge of a hill offering various intricately layered views of the city. At one point sitting down you look out over a low curved wall shaped like a bowl, a beautiful downward curve, through which you see the curve, an upward curve, of the edge of the garden itself, which is the exact mirror opposite of the curve of the wall, and beyond that the curve of the hill beyond the city, which it perfectly mocks — and everywhere there are such intricate visual plays. Here Dad has his first angina attack on the trip — sits down in the sculpture garden to wait out the pain, later he sits in the Museum while we go through the exhibition of antiquities — ancient pots, artifacts, sarcophagi, masks, etc. of civilizations in this area that go back long before the time of Abraham. Israel was already an ancient civilization at the time of Christ — Roman times must have seemed quite advanced, modern, decadent.

Isamu Noguchi is possessed of a subtle Japanese appreciation of the delicate beauty of the visible. I remember a work of his I saw once in New York: a big round stone, flattened on top, and rigged up with a fountain inside. Water comes up from the hidden fountain very very slowly, imperceptibly, covering the top of the rock like a mirror and flowing over the sides into stones below so slowly you can't tell if it's flowing or not.

Once I met Mr. Noguchi at Zentatsu Baker's house. Zentatsu is distinguished by the fact that he knows many famous people. He tells you about the various famous people he knows and you don't believe he could really know all these people, it is rather mysterious how he knows them all, but every once in a while one of them actually appears, and so it did not surprise me much that once when Zentatsu and I were deep in conversation about his favorite topic at that time: what had happened to him and the Zen Center, how to explain it what to do about it, the doorbell rang and it was Isamu Noguchi paying an unscheduled call. He was just passing through on some business and proposed that he stay the night, as he apparently often did when in San Francisco.

It is a fond memory of mine: Zentatsu and I collaborating to make the bed for Isamu as he sat on the chair in the bedroom explaining everything to us. I remember the sheet billowing up and floating onto the bed. It was very unusual because Zentatsu did not at that time make beds very often, and although he and I had been very close as teacher and student in another way we didn't know each other at all and had never before nor since shared such a fine moment preparing a bed for the comfort of another person.

Isamu had lost his luggage on the airplane. I explained to him that he needn't worry because they will bring it to him as soon as it comes in on the next plane. They almost never actually lose it. After that Zentatsu contrived to get me out of the room and told me not to be so stupid, Isamu Noguchi knew perfectly well all about luggage on airplanes since he practically lived on airplanes all the time taking care of his various projects and studios all over the world. I had recently lost my luggage for the first time on my flight to Vancouver, so I was full of this new information about what happens when you lose your luggage on the airplane, but I could see it was pretty stupid to tell this to Isamu Noguchi.

I was impressed with the elegance of the speech of Isamu Noguchi and with his demeanor. You could see immediately that he was one of the great men of our century and had known many of the other great men of our century. It was interesting to talk with him and to listen to him. It seems the project he was interested in had to do with building a huge monument and lowering it onto Alcatraz Island, a really huge monument in the shape of a pyramid, if I remember correctly, bigger than any other monument anywhere. It did sound really exciting and worthwhile as he described it. So far there is no good use for Alcatraz Island. But it would take a great deal of persuasion and negotiation to bring this thing about.

Another important part of the Israel Museum is the Shrine of the Book, a building in the shape of the lids of the pottery jars in which the Dead Sea Scrolls were found (the jars themselves are on display in the building). The building lowers fifty feet into the ground in case of a bombing attack.

The Dead Sea scrolls were found in 1947 by a Bedouin boy in caves near Qumran. They include first century B.C. writings of the Essene sect, a proto-Christian Jewish group of monastics, doubtless precursors doctrinally and in lifestyle of the Christian movements (they seem to have invented the mass and the baptism, a logical outgrowth of the Jewish penchant for cleanliness and ritual purity). Reading Edmund Wilson's book on the subject — very interesting. It gives a sense of the gradual organic development of Christianity out of the tendency of Judaism for final apocalyptic solutions and terrible symbolism, the consequence of imagining that time has a beginning and a final goal, God a final purpose, and that language can unlock its secret. The world seen as a book written in very large enigmatic letters that describes this secret if only we could decipher it.

The scrolls are displayed in a circular room along with photos of the excavations at Qumran and artifacts found there — ritual

cups, wool blankets, pots, mirrors, and so on- the writing committed on what looks like thin cloth pages stitched together,
remarkably well preserved and readable (they were wrapped up in
the urns and sealed with beeswax).

JERUSALEM AGAIN
(AGAIN)

WE ARE STANDING ON THE ROOF of the Old City of Jerusalem. Since many of the suqs have roofs over them, much of the city is enclosed, and you can climb some steps to the roof and look down over the edge to the open streets in four directions to see the four quarters of the city, Moslem, Jewish, Christian, Armenian. Just now the Moslem call to prayer begins to blare through the loudspeakers — a strange wailing sound that completely charges the atmosphere — and is completely ignored by our Jewish tour guide, whose basic subject seems to be the courage and destiny of the Jew versus the barbarism of the Moslem (the Christians seem to be more or less irrelevant). See, he says, pointing down at the tastefully renovated Jewish quarter on the one side and the ramshackle crowded Arab quarter on the other side.

The tour took us to the ruins of the Hurva synagogue which, like most of the Jewish quarter, was destroyed in '48 when the Jews here surrendered to the Arabs and evacuated this quarter they had inhabited for so many centuries. The Arabs then made a point of destroying everything, especially the synagogues, which have not been rebuilt, their ruins serving as a reminder of this Arab outrage. But most of the rest of the quarter has been rebuilt, using new stone on top of old, and everywhere this combination of new and old is apparent (and is an explicit theme of our tour guide, who is terribly proud of it, and it is no doubt a theme of the nation). No escaping the present Jewish quarter as a really high-class shopping mall on the theme of Jewish/Roman antiquities, with gratings in the sidewalk here and there, for peering down into excavations, or balconies from which you can look down onto clean stone passageways lined with modern shops between the Roman columns. The intricacies of the various periods and the several layers of architecture interrelated is preserved here, and our guide offers explanations of the scope of the intricacies and explains the very complicated architectural keys through the reading of which one (but not me) can decipher it all. The guide, I think he is a recent Russian emigrant, is very impressed by this, the whole project is so new and exciting, this part of the City has only been in Jewish hands since the victory of '67, the work is still going on, new things discovered every day, the Cardo, built by the Romans, which was in fact an ancient shopping mall, was unearthed only a few years ago, now you can see the columns reconstructed, and the original stones of the street, the drainage system, the Roman aesthetic of heavy handed straightforward clear cut planning using bold straight lines — a wide street right smack through the middle of the city end to end.

After the tour of the Jewish quarter we wandered around the Old City for a while longer in and out of streets as different as nations, one minute in a crowded suq where are displayed skinned calf heads and pig brains amid shouting crowds donkeys and darting kids, next minute, turn a corner, and on a quiet street full of shops selling Christian memorabilia, monks in robes quietly going by, until by chance we came to the Church of the Holy Sepulcher, built on the very spot where Jesus was crucified, anointed, and buried. It is somehow pretty hard to believe this is actually the spot; like other such momentous historical occurrences it is hard to pinpoint a precise location for the event, impossible to say, not knowing exactly seems to be the essence of such an event, its real meaning, yet millions of pilgrims seem to know it's so, flock here in the millions, though scholars, who don't know for sure, list two or three really good theories of where Golgotha might actually have been.

The church is dark, clammy, somewhat creepy, straining toward a kind of crypt-like glory but not reaching it. We sit down on a bench next to some kind of Christian brother in sneakers and habit who looks to be overweight and in terrible health, barely breathing, to look at our guidebook which quotes Melville's journals to the effect that this church is clammy and overrated.

Near our bench, close to the entrance, is a salmon-colored stone slab about the size of a human body: the very spot where Jesus was anointed after his removal from the Cross. Going around to the left we come to a small chapel — very dark inside, which is the very location of his burial place. Because the doorway is very low you have to bend your head to get into the shadowy anteroom and you can't get into the tiny darkened inner room at all without kneeling (the ceiling is about four and a half feet high). Women in black are on their knees in there huddled around candles singing. Their faces look really beatific in the candlelight, infused with the enthusiasm and otherworldly presence of Christ. Each of them seems to be beside herself; they are beside each other; they are looking at something you can't see from outside the room.

We followed the crowd around and up some steps to a large altar under which is a box that opens down through the floor to the actual spot where the Cross stood. You can go up and put your hand right into there, which I did.

The great complicated story of this church has to do with the rivalry between the various sects who each claim the church as their turf. Compromises have been effected which divide the responsibility and privilege, but no one has been entirely satisfied with this arrangement and an uneasy truce prevails. This is why the church remains mixed up, repair work always going on, and mismanaged.

Down in the basement there is an inscribed stone that has lately been excavated. Thousands of hours of high powered study have produced the conclusion that this stone was placed here by a pilgrim probably only a few decades after the Crucifixion — proof positive that this is in fact the place.

It's pretty dark down here and not many tourists have bothered to come down this far to see the stone.

I look at the stone, pondering the difference, if there is any as far as I am concerned, between the actual time and place of Christ's crucifixion, my imagination of that time and place, and this time and place.

MA'ALEH HAMISHMA

WE MISSED THE BUS TO MA'ALEH HAMISHMA so we tried to get a
cab. Jeff hailed one cab and asked for a price, while Dad hailed
another one and asked the price (we are suspicious of cabbies).
After a little bit of confusion we finally got into one of the cabs,
but the other cabby became furious, leaped out of his cab and
stood between us and the first cab, preventing us from entering.
The first cabby gets out of his cab and the two of them (I think
one of them is an Ashkenazi one a Sephardi, or perhaps one of
them is an Arab) get into a shouting match, one cabby, the
furious one, has yellowish eyes, he really looks like he's liable to
pull out a gun or a knife at any moment, finally we just say look,
forget it, and walk away. By now several people have gathered —
finally the first cab makes a U turn on the wide street and follows
us down the street, picks us up, and we are on our way to
Ma'aleh Hamishma, the nearby Kibbutz where Michelle lives.

Michelle is my cousin Marvin's daughter who has managed,
against her father's initial protests, apparently, to marry Roi, a
kibbutznik from Ma'aleh Hamishma.

We wander around looking for her house along a row of little
rundown houses that, as we discover, were at one time chicken
houses. Things are very quiet here. It reminds me a lot of Green

58

Gulch, wholesome but slightly unkempt, no one is concerned with property values because no one owns anything. Very different feeling from Jerusalem where everything is spruced up and modern (excluding areas near the Old City walls which were border territory before the '67 war, and excluding, of course, sections where many Arabs live). This is an old Kibbutz, one of the early ones (1938).

Michelle gives us a tour— the children's houses, one for each age group, the dairy farm, automatic milking, in the distance the completely modernized chicken yard. Looking out from the hill of the dairy you can see across the valley a hill with a war monument on it — this is "ammunition hill" where there was heavy fighting during the '67 war. Now it is covered with houses — a new West Bank settlement. She takes us to the dining room where tonight (Shabbat) they will light candles and read from Sefer Torah, but otherwise no religious observances will be held: on Shabbat, unlike other nights, they set the table. She takes us to a mural that depicts, in typical socialist realist heroic style, the founding of the kibbutz. One of the founders is Roi's uncle. Five of them were killed in an early Arab ambush — they are depicted handing up their tools to the younger generation as they pass down into darkness.

Michelle is a pert pretty young woman, short and plump, cheerful and happy, recently mother of her second son (we go to one children's house first for her to feed Oren, her youngest, then to another house to get Amin, her two year old). She describes the bureaucracy and pettiness of Kibbutz life — jealousy over her getting a fancy baby carriage from her rich American father, difficulty in getting permission to go to the states to visit family etc. — it all sounds very familiar, very much like home in my own community. But, like Moishe and Panina, who complain cheerfully about the lunacy of Israeli life, Michelle is on the whole happy — she finds meaning and purpose here that she could not find in the USA. She misses America and can't really adjust to some things — her kids not knowing her native culture, the gossip, which she calls the backbone of kibbutz life, not enough time to spend with her family (the basic six-day work week — and then the necessity for everyone to "give" one Saturday a month); and the "unreality" of war, and the army routine (every man has to go forty days a year for reserve duty till age fifty-five — and the wars do happen; Roi's older brother was paralyzed in the 1967 war; his oldest brother has fought in two wars).

Though the Kibbutz is leftist and non-religious all marriages and ceremonies are done according to the Orthodox tradition — an Orthodox rabbi comes in to do them. We're standing overlooking the village of Abu Ghosh, on the other side of the Kibbutz — a friendly Israeli-Arab village that sends workers to the Kibbutz to help. Some years ago followers of Mayer Kahane, the outspoken American-born Israeli anti-Arab racist, later a Knesset member, and ultimately assassinated, made a demonstration there and wrote obscenities and curses on the walls. Young people from the Kibbutz went down to clean up and paint. And yet, according to Michelle, even these people — you never know — people who've seen Roi grow up — could one day turn around and knife him. You can't be sure. Michelle's attitudes seem to be given to her by the Kibbutz — the accepted attitude. They do not necessarily seem to be hers. Politics is not my thing, she says.

One disturbing and constant aspect of things here is that Israelis definitely believe that Arabs are essentially bad, stupid, unreliable, incapable people who want to kill us. Could this actually be true? Does believing it tend to make it continually true? Is it foolish, suicidal, not to believe it?

Waiting for her to feed Oren we sit under pine trees in the children's house yard drinking cold water and talk about Russia — my cousin Lloyd made a recent trip there. Dad points out there's no cars on the street there, people have to wait in long lines. Lloyd found it not so bad but Dad told him they're not showing him the real stuff. I point out they have almost no unemployment, everyone is guaranteed a place to live, medical care, etc. In the USA we have homelessness, slums, and palaces. It all boils down to this, Dad says, these kibbutzim are practically communistic!

At the children's house we meet Roi, a great big jovial but serious man with a steady gaze and large lips and teeth, so that his smile is quite an event — I am immediately impressed with his presence that expresses courtesy and capability and wonder at Marvin's opinion of him as a guy who doesn't like to study, isn't exactly bright, may not be the perfect husband, and so on. Yet, it seems to me, here's a guy you could clearly trust with your life, your kibbutz, that he would steadily care for it, would know what to do in any circumstance.

We talk politics at the kibbutz pool. The West Bank is a bargaining chip for peace, Roi says. But what about all the settlers, I say, thinking of Simon, Hilda, Moishe, Panina, and their children. Some of the biggest towns they won't give up maybe, but there may be something we can give up. This is very complicated. I have to look at a map. The Labor Party has always been in favor of peace for many years, even though it was Likud who signed the first treaty with Egypt, when we gave up the Sinai. I really miss the Sinai, he says, by way of arguing that since he was willing to give it up perhaps others might be willing to give up the West Bank. It was the one place you could go to get away from it all, when you wanted to forget everything, he says. You could go to the Sinai to forget. The country is so small, everyone always on top of you, but there was always the Sinai. I say I have not heard this viewpoint from other Israelis, he says when you go up to Eyn Hashofet there you'll hear it. In the car on the way back to Jerusalem he talks further about the kibbutz movement. Once idealized by the Israeli population it is today the butt of jealousy — kibbutzim are considered wealthy and arrogant. Many other kinds of small communities founded in the last twenty years have not been able to do as well. Kibbutzim have had a head start and have been successful, so many are jealous. And the kibbutz movement became rich — we had a lot of what do you call it — assets.

But some big shot invested it all — eighty million dollars — in bad investments, with some kind of crook, and now it's gone. That guy is probably working in the chicken house now. Kibbutzim are going more toward industrialization — we don't on principle hire cheap labor, so we can't grow vegetables, not profitably, only cotton, livestock. But we will never stop farming. Why? Because we have the land and we are not going to sell it, so we have to do something with it. Roi is studying business management at the Kibbutz University where he has to live four days a week. He plans to come back to the kibbutz to work after he completes the two-year course, but even now he "gives" two days a week work to the kibbutz in the chicken house sorting eggs which is maybe a good thing to clear the mind, to break the routine, he says. Roi feels that the schooling he is receiving now will enable him to manage the kibbutz well and that it is manageable and that their solution would be a hell of a lot easier if only the Likud with its hysterical supporters would fade away and the Labor Party had a chance to deal with the situation. He seems very clear about all of this.

RACISM

A FEW DAYS AGO IT DAWNED ON ME that most of the people in this world are victims of racism or perpetrators of racism or, very often, both. Of course, I already knew that there was racism here and there and that it is a problem, but I had not realized before that the overwhelming majority of humans are involved with racism. People who believe that it is desirable, righteous, possible, to see all people as worthy and to treat all people with respect and care are actually vastly in the minority.

It dawned on me suddenly as I was walking on top of a hill looking at a tree. The tree, it was a pine tree, was just standing there, crooked, very tall, very dignified, very present, unmoving in the wind. I was really shocked, and I nearly started to cry.

A few educated white well to do people in the United States or in Europe and other people not educated and not white I'm sure here and there all over the world may believe that people are all worthy of respect and should be treated with respect, but actually of course most of us do not act on this even though we may think we believe it, and certainly the implications of the way we live obviate this belief of ours, even if we think we are acting on it.

There are of course a lot of examples of people who have acted out lives that were totally unprejudiced and proactively kind. But these people have generally been regarded as saints. In other words, freaks.

All over the world, Africa, Asia, America, Europe, it is not at all clear to people that it is desirable, righteous or possible to see all kinds of people as worthy of respect and to make a serious effort to treat them that way.

The world used to be divided into East and West, cut in half by Churchill's "Iron Curtain," the Free World and the Communist World they used to call it when I was growing up. At that time it didn't look like there were that many distinct kinds of people. Just two kinds. And that the differences between these kinds had to do with what each one believed. But as the conceptual grid of these great historical divisions slowly lifted up into the air off of the various people running around on the earth it became clear that there are all these different kinds of people and that they have had complex and often destructive relations with one another over a long period of time. The many tribes in Africa, the many tribes in Vietnam, Cambodia, the many ethnic groups in China, Russia, Eastern Europe, the many nationalities in America, the Greeks and the Turks, the Catholics and Protestants in Ireland, the Christians and Moslems in Lebanon, the Moslems and Hindus in India, the Navajo and the Hopi, Sephardi and Ashkenazi, Arab and Jew, French and German, and so on, and between these various groups there are great traditional hatreds that have been created by actual things that have happened in the past so horrible that to forget them would be a betrayal of one's own blood and so the force of them goes on.

To talk to these various people about how they should love one another or treat one other with respect is stupid. They will tell you that it is very fine for you to suggest this but you do not really know what you are talking about because if I try to trust them they will betray me or kill me or worse. Telling me to respect them or love them is like telling me I have three legs or two heads. It is certainly fine for you to talk about this and give speeches about it but for certain if you would be in the conditions I have been in and see what I have seen, the loss of my home, of my wife and daughter, father and husband, of my arms and legs, of my business, my land, the burial place of my ancestors, then I do not think it would really be that easy for you to speak of these things in the way that you speak of them now.

As I think about all of this it is nearly the middle of the last decade of this millennium. And I wonder whether in the next millennium there will be as much killing of people by people as there has been in this one. Our language, our notions, our thoughts and feelings, only go so far. I think there must be a way of thinking, a way of living, that we can now not even imagine, a jump in evolution perhaps that is like growing another leg or another arm. Or maybe we can imagine this new way of living, maybe we already have imagined it in our religious imagination only we haven't made it real yet. Because it takes first of all an awakening, and then a commitment, and then a lot of work, in order to realize it.

One of my best friends is the poet and Zen priest Philip Whalen. We have known each other a long time and most of what I know about how to write poetry I learned from him. A few months ago we were driving through San Francisco and he was telling me about a recent trip he'd made to Germany to help lead a week-long Zen retreat. I was really surprised at how I reacted, he said. I don't know what happened but suddenly I looked around the room and realized that there weren't any Jews in the zendo. I am used to Jews in the zendo, wherever I practice there are a lot of Jews. And then I realized why there weren't any Jews in the zendo: they had all been killed, there weren't any Jews here anymore. And I started to cry and I cried through the whole retreat. And I could feel it everywhere, I could see it in the landscape, in the trees, I could hear it in the names of all the places. I thought I had forgotten about that, that it was all a long time ago. But it was still there.

We were on our way to a Chinese restaurant to have lunch as he was telling me this. Phil loves to go out to lunch, he loves to eat all kinds of lovely food, and he loves books, and music, and flowers, and he hates cant and obscurity and sentimentality. The city's streets, and San Francisco is a very lovely city, with beautiful streets, and a powerful open bright sunlight, zipped past as we drove along; over the rims of the hills there were glimpses of the bay with sailboats on it. And Phil was quietly weeping.

A few weeks after that Phil and I went out to breakfast with another poet friend, Leslie Scalapino, who had recently been to Russia. She said she was really surprised, in talking to the most Westernized avant-garde poets, to find that they were quite completely and quite casually anti-Semitic. There was one though, Arcaadi Dragomaschenko, who wasn't that way at all. He seemed to have no prejudices at all, even against his comrades who were quite prejudiced. At one point, Leslie said, Arcaadi was being interviewed by a French journalist who remarked that he seemed very unusual compared to anyone else the journalist had met in Russia. You actually seem happy, the journalist had said. Arcaadi translated this exchange for Leslie and asked her if she could make any sense of it. Because it didn't make a bit of sense to him.

WHITE BLACK YELLOW
PINK BROWN TAN READ

Israelis now in the position for Israelis
Palestinians throw rocks in the street are shot
Is South Africans shot running with their backs to the
guns
The white is not white anymore he is pink he can't go
to the bank
To eat sushi without the black at the back shoves with
a bark
Yet the black is not black he is brown or tan he looks
broad, rounded he is not
                   night anymore than the white is
day, foggy day
No mansion without devastation no extensive flower border
without a hovel behind a slat fence under cover of a busted tree
The chair is warmer after the cat gets up and chaos follows
                release
Damage riot murder grief surely ensue, the
                    first step leads on
Fairfax, Kentfield, Mill Valley, Ross, cities of Marin
The Israeli army orders fiberglass clubs when wooden
truncheons break too frequently smashing Arab heads cutting
the hands of the soldiers

These boys and girls are not monsters are not crude it
is only logical
As shining hope and dream sink naturally into the sea
at evening like the sun does at sunset as seabirds call
A moral imperative weighs in each sip of margarita in
each step and thump of Reebok Court Shoe
700 kids shot at
Soweto running away with their backs to the guns kids
dancing
Sweet with the exultation of a moment's belief in a wider and
more beautiful
       Future
Fairfax Belvedere Larkspur Tiburon
A dangerous position to be spun in a direction in which
election ordains the back as front
Front as back, justifies through blindness paranoia
Israeli settlers knock over photographers punch the faces
of photographers' spouses push cameras into their eyebrows
Only a few years ago Israeli settlers killed by Palestinians
at the edge of kibbutz
                          hand down tractors to sons to put in
irrigation pipe build the long chicken houses tend
the cotton fields
The South African landscape's like this one rolling hills
mountains streams
In Manchuria the Japanese had the Chinese dig pits before
which to kneel as they shot them
And the Germans and Russians have also done this to the
Jews and Russians and Germans
The shopping Center north of Corte Madera is designed
to look like the town I grew up in and the next shopping center
up the highway
Looks like a quaint Spanish settlement of two hundred
years ago
There are whole stores devoted to popcorn, sporting goods,

gifts, light fixtures, convenient storage containers for your closets,

Nine kinds of pens imported from Japan where during the war there was little rice to eat and at the end of the war

Many suffered the effects of nuclear fire. The Israeli soldiers check the bags of all who enter the pavilion

Where the Kotel stands and once a day or so an innocent-looking backpack is left by mistake by a tourist

And the area is cleared for the bomb squad. The Irish also kill the Irish or the English to make a point

The Lebanese, Christians, kill the Lebanese, Moslems, and the Sikhs blow up in the Hindus in the monasteries

Creative work self-expression a determination to achieve sufficiency and art

that cannot be denied

People are enthusiastic for the material a symphony lurching forward to its foreordained conclusion muffled in silence

These are the martyrs, bodhisattvas, and it would be a woeful mistake to expect results today

Or at any other time. Rather it is a song like a single straight railroad track of melody extends forever

Straight into and through the fabric of time like a baby cries an old man dies endings are nothing to be anxious about effort goes on

Indefinitely offered as if sky into time as if night

It is a situation that cannot obtain forever because volition inheres, weighs down

Now is the time, here the place.

ARABS AND JEWS

F ROM FODOR'S *ISRAEL, 1987, TRAVEL GUIDE*:

"For purposes of convenience, the two major groups of Jews are known as Ashkenazim and Sephardim. Technically, the Ashkenazim are the descendants of those Jews who originally went to Germany (Ashkenaz in medieval Hebrew) and later spread out throughout Central and Eastern Europe. They spoke Yiddish, a language largely derived from German, but with many Hebrew and Slavic words and written in Hebrew letters. Later, they formed the major Jewish communities in Western Europe and the US.

"The Sephardim, strictly speaking, are the descendants of those Jews who were exiled from Spain (Sepharad in Hebrew) in the 15th century and who mostly found refuge in the then more tolerant Muslim East. They spoke Ladino, a language close to medieval Spanish and also written in Hebrew letters. But just to make things confusing, some Sephardim settled in England, Holland, the Americas and even Germany. And to make it even more confusing, in Israel today all Jews of Middle Eastern origin are known collectively as Sephardim, even though their ancestors never stepped on Spanish soil.

"Within these two subdivisions, the ethnic mixture is almost infinite. There are Kurdish Jews, who, in addition to speaking the

Arabic and Kurdish of their non-Jewish neighbors, spoke Aramaic among themselves, the language of the Jews at the time of Jesus. There are Georgian Jews, not from the American South, but from the Asian Soviet republic. (In Jerusalem there's a community of Jews from Boukhara, also in Soviet Asia, who in the last century were known for their wealth. Men and women dressed in gorgeously embroidered robes. Then Soviet Russia conquered Boukhara and they were suddenly cut off from their source of income, leaving them impoverished, but still boasting their fine robes and, often as not, palatial homes.) The small Indian Jewish community traces its origins back thousands of years. Like the rest of Indian society, the Jews of India were divided into several sub-groups.

"When they arrived in Israel in the early '50s, one group would barely speak to the other.

"Each community of immigrants has its own traditions, customs, dress and foods. But even in less than four decades these have often become confused and intermingled. Thus, the Moroccan Jews have a popular holiday at the end of Passover, the Mimouna. In Morocco families would go out together for a day in the countryside. Now, in Israel, the day has evolved into a huge outdoor picnic attended by Israelis of every background.

"Nor should it be thought for a moment that all Jews of European origin are alike. The Hungarians are known for their distinctive accent, and their prowess in cake making, the Germans for their cultural and academic distinction, and the fact that despite this many of them seem incapable of learning Hebrew. The early pioneers from Russia still hold the upper hand, politically, while those who have come from Russia in the last few decades are often ready to dismiss other Israelis, including the earlier immigrants from Russia, as 'uncultured primitives.' And if you meet someone of Romanian origin, he will no doubt happily tell you that all (other) Romanians are thieves.

"Meanwhile, in recent years yet another ethnic group has made its presence felt. These are immigrants from the English-speaking world. Semites they may be, but they are generally somewhat startled on arrival to hear themselves described as 'Anglo Saxons.' Nonetheless, this is how they are commonly known in Israel. (To be fair, a representative sample of these 'Anglo Saxons' will often as not include the odd Dutchman or Scandinavian.) Many of these English-speakers, used to the more delicate social courtesies of their countries of origin, are often put out by the more abrasive approach in Israel. Some adapt, many never do — but some of those nice 'Anglo-Saxon' manners have begun to rub off on the natives as well.

"Like the Jews, Israel's non-Jews, though mostly Arab, are far from one ethnic unity. About 80 per cent are Muslim Arabs, but even among them there is a sharp differentiation between those who live in cities and villages and the Bedouins, many of whom still wander through the wilderness with their flocks. In political terms, many of the Israeli Arabs identify with Arab nationalism, while the Bedouins have no qualms about expressing their support for a Jewish state and often volunteer to serve as trusted and valued members of the Israeli army.

"Distinct from the Muslims, although their religion is said to be an offshoot of Islam, are over 50,000 Druze, a fierce group of mountain dwellers in the Galilee, part of a larger community spread through Syria and Lebanon. Known for their bravery on the battlefield, their men are drafted, like Jews, into the army and often serve with distinction. But their firm allegiance to the State of Israel has been tested in recent years as a result of the war in Lebanon when Druze soldiers from Israel sometimes found themselves in confrontation with the Druze of Lebanon.

"Intriguingly, the Druze religion, which apparently began in the tenth century A.D. is secret and only chosen members are introduced to all its mysteries. What is known is that they revere Jethro, the father-in-law of Moses, and make a yearly pilgrimage to his tomb in the Galilee. With sweeping mustaches for the men and gauzy white head scarves for the women, they make up one of Israel's more colorful groups.

"Nor can we forget the Circassians, Muslims from the Caucasus Mountains. They settled in two villages in the Galilee in the nineteenth century, after their country had been conquered by Russia, yet retain their language and much of their Slavic tradition. Here, too, a martial tradition is expressed through service in the army."

MASADA

Israel is the land of tour buses. Egged (pronounced "Egg, Ed") is the name of the tour bus company that will take you everywhere and explain everything to you and along the way give you some gentle but pointed political point of view about the current situation in Israel. Nothing in Israel is unrelated to issues of war and peace and survival; everything is an argument, an intense struggle for viewpoint, a confinement of articulation. That's what it has always been to be a Jew, I suppose: to engage continually in the fundamental discourse about the right, the necessity, the justification of the right, and the necessity, to be. You can't just be there, just there just like that. You have to discuss, confute, cajole, enjoin. That's how it is. Especially here. This is where the argument begins and ends. Because God gives you a place and it's yours.

The bus always picks you up at the hotel and all of us middle-aged and elderly Jewish people pile on cheerfully yet not without a certain anxiety — is the luggage stowed properly, did we bring what we need, do we have a hat. A woman, about thirty-five, very fat, very exasperated and talkative, wearing really big earrings made with shocks of white goat's hair, is blocking the aisle with a big suitcase as everyone begins to board. A lot of jostling and

74

grumbling as people try to find ways to get around her. She seems particularly disorganized in an erratic sort of way — or at least a way different from the way most of us are disorganized: she seems to be the embodiment of disorganization itself, with no cover story. The sight of such a creature is of course immediately upsetting, especially when you are about to set off on a journey in a place where there may be danger, there are definitely no Howard Johnsons, and you don't know what the weather will be, and she is prolonging the anticipation. No one knows what to do with her, but finally one of the tour bus company dispatchers, a large man in cheap clothing with a look of resignation and exasperation on his face, gets onto the bus. He seems to know this woman and to be perfectly patiently though unhappily aware of her debilities. It seems she wants to get a hat and an umbrella out of her enormous suitcase. After all it will be very hot in the sun at Masada. The man waits for her to do this, then hoists her suitcase off the bus and into the luggage compartment below, and we are off.

The bus trip includes a viewpoint on the heroic and historical geography of the Holy Land, down from the foothills of Jerusalem and into the fertile Hebron Valley, the country of the Patriarchs, the land where Abraham walked, settled, had children, and it was here too that Moses, coming back to the land after the first exile (the first of so many) sent spies to see what the land was like, who lived there, how easily they could be overcome. This area is part of the West Bank, territories that were on the Arab side of the 1949 cease fire border, were not part of the original state of Israel whose shape on the map I memorized as a kid (the West Bank is the bite taken out on the western side). And so all these villages we pass are Arab villages, and beside the road sometimes we see the high walls of the refugee camps. Our tour guide, an American expatriate, an owly sixtyish man wearing olive drab Banana Republic pants (which feature zippers around the legs above the thighs, so they can be converted into shorts), assures us as we pass through the town of Bethlehem, that these villages in

75

what some call "occupied territory" and he calls "administrative territories" are actually quite free to do as they please. They elect their own mayors and run their own affairs more or less — the Israeli military governors are only on hand to assist in the process, if need be, he tells us. The bus passes into the open countryside where rocky hills have been terrace-farmed by peasant peoples since the beginning of history — rocks plucked from the soil piled up to make walls that retain the earth to hold moisture and prevent erosion. Good grape growing country here, like the south of France or the Napa Valley in California, tough clay soil, little rainfall, cold winters, grapes, about sixty thousand tons of them a year our guide tells us, are grown primitively — bush grapes, pole-trained grapes, grapes on vines that hug the ground, all sorts of grapes, but none for wine, because Muslims don't use alcohol. Once in a while we see a farmer going by with a donkey.

We stop at a village beyond Hebron that is known for its glass blowing. Everyone piles out of the bus to watch the glassblowers work and then to buy everything passionately at this scheduled buy-everything stop. There is great controversy and anxiety always about shopping, which is the major element of travel for many people. Not to miss the never to be repeated opportunity to bring home the good thing, yet not to make the mistake of paying too much — especially to these Arab craftsmen who might be cheating you just because you are Jewish and American and therefore they think wealthy. Add to this the strict schedule the bus must keep to get us to Masada on time, and there is a great hubbub and trouble in the glassblowing shop. I find shopping the great ordeal of travel. You want to buy everything and nothing, the prices are all too high and they seem at the same time very reasonable. Value becomes quite arbitrary and the currency doesn't make sense. Money takes on a different meaning when you travel — it is even more irrational than usual. But clearly on the scheduled buy-everything stop on the Egg, Ed bus tour, when everyone is buying everything it is impossible also not to buy and so I buy something that I think smashed in my suitcase on the return trip.

We pass through more fertile hills, a forest of Aleppo pine and cedar, settlements where all kinds of fruit trees grow, very organized and productive. I do not now remember the name of these settlements which began as military outposts in which farming work is done, and then when the soldiers end their military service they stay on, trained now not only as farmers but also as defenders of land. It is a good economic opportunity, and it is one of the many ways the government encourages the securing of Israeli enclaves within these territories.

Gradually the fertile hills give way to green lush fields on the outskirts of the city of Beer-Sheba, which means seven wells, or possibly "oath at the well," so named in the times of Abraham during a water dispute. Today Beer-Sheba is a town of over one hundred thousand, and seems quite prosperous. Our guide tells us that here some of the Bedouins have taken up irrigation and property, left off migration and sheep, and have become very wealthy. The Bedouins we see in the Negev and elsewhere seem to wander around a bit aimlessly, living in army green tents that whip in the desert winds as does the rubbish that seems to scatter all around them and their sheep.

We take another buy-everything stop outside town at a Bedouin market, a teeming place with endless stalls selling mainly the same junky stuff one finds nearly everywhere in the world now — a grandiose flea market. Just off the bus I am accosted by a Bedouin man selling burnoose — the cloth and headdress. He puts them on me. How wonderful they look! I make you a good price. He starts at twenty shekel, I say my price is ten, walk along, he follows me: ten, nine, eight, seven, six, at five I take out my wallet and he sells me the cotton (I hope) characteristic gray and white cloth, but not the headdress, I don't want the headdress, then he grabs the cloth out of my hand and hands me another, larger, of nicer quality. Give me ten more shekel and take this one, this one is much better, the other is no good, you can't wash it, it will fall apart!

Onward through ever deepening desert, past tan hills and buttes encircled by wadis through which furious waterways run in winter. A long descent this way — landscape carved seemingly so violently, yet so quiet, bright, seemingly nothing alive here, nothing stirs, here and there caves blown into thick swirled shapes — to the Dead Sea, 1,380 feet below sea level, lowest spot on earth. The sea is vast and completely calm, the water does not move, bluish in the haze of evaporated water that makes everything look fuzzy and mirage-like, dotted on this side with what look like whitecaps but closer up are seen to be salt deposits rising above the water's surface. It is not possible to write too many words about — and my ability to describe is not equal to — the power of this landscape, the feeling of starkness, desolation, power, amazement, nothingness one is assailed by here — out of which not only Christ, but all of his precursors emerged, desert of the mind and of the spirit, but not desert — there is hot sand. Stone. Cliff. Sun. Of a single color in the haze. And on to Masada.

Dad, Jeff and I take the cable car up to the top of this fortress on top of a cliff, heady, dizzy, like walking around on the moon, without a tree, a bush, a plant anywhere in sight. What mind, what notion in that mind, conceived the idea of putting what amounted to a royal village up here? Herod, mighty king of the Jews who as far as I can tell must have been a character whose arrogance (to think he could build this thing in the first place) was matched only by his paranoia (to think he had to build it in case the Jews, on the one hand, or the Romans, on the other, drove him out of Jerusalem). The setting is a tremendous plateau several thousand feet above ground level. Here Herod had all manner of luxurious palaces and baths and walkways constructed, and an entire village that would support the royal entourage. After Herod's time Masada was abandoned but taken by the Zealots in A.D.66, at the end of the Great Revolt against Rome. The Zealots were messianic freedom fighters who believed passionately and fanatically that it was absolutely wrong to live under Roman rule. Under siege for years, the 960 Zealots in Masada were ultimately the last free Jews to face the Romans. Several legions (about eight thousand men) opposed them, and from up here you can look down and see the outlines of the Roman encampments below, small villages in themselves, squares marked by piles of rubble. To the east you can see the outlines of footpaths trailing off toward Jerusalem which the Romans used for transportation of supplies (somehow the Zealots managed to be self sufficient — growing crops up here irrigated with what little rainwater could be caught in cisterns; eating the vast supplies of food sealed in jars that miraculously survived the two hundred years since Herod). To the west is, rounded now, the dirt ramp the Romans built — from ground level all the way up to here, it must have taken years, thousands of Jewish slaves captured during the Revolt did the work, day by day the Zealots looking down and watching the work's progress, and no doubt doing all they could to stop it. The ramp made it possible for the Romans finally to put their siege tower into operation, battering at Masada's walls till they fell, then torching the hastily-built wooden walls built behind them, and then, the next day, barging in to find everyone already dead. According to Josephus (who wrote the eyewitness account of the Great Revolt, a book called *The Jewish Wars*) the men drew lots and ten men were chosen to kill everyone, and one to kill the last nine before killing himself. This was in A.D. 73, three years after the Revolt had ended.

Masada then became a Roman outpost, then a Christian monastery, but it was abandoned in 300 and forgotten entirely for over a thousand years. In 1962 the great Israeli soldier-archeologist Yigael Yadin assembled from all over the world an army of volunteers to restore Masada, and today, in the heat, we walk among the rebuilt walls of storerooms, synagogues, we view the mosaics on the walls of Herod's palace.

Most members of Israeli tank divisions are sworn in as members of the army up here. Holding a Bible in one hand a rifle in the other they take the pledge, "A second time Masada will not fall!"

Wandering around up here, looking down and imagining the Romans massed below, trying to think about the spirit of the Zealots, stubborn thorns in the side of the Romans (no one else in the Empire dared revolt and there wasn't really all that much reason to revolt), thorns in the side of the Poles, the Russians, the Germans, the English, the Arabs.

The sun reflected off all this rock evacuates the mind, burns the feeling of Masada in right through the eyes.

TIME AND SPACE

THESE DAYS I KEEP A CALENDAR in which I write down things that I will do in the future — trips to take, various Zen retreats, workshops, classes to give, poetry readings, meetings. Then I plan out the events and then they come around, I do whatever it is that I seem to be required to do, then it is over, I cross it off my list, then more come. While all this is going on even though I don't notice much, I am getting older all the time, very quickly there is less life ahead of me than there was, and more life behind me than there was.

Sometimes I stop what I am doing and consider the strangeness of time's passage. I am supposed to be a certain age, it is supposed to be a certain year. But it doesn't actually feel that way sometimes. Of course I know it is that way; but also sometimes it isn't.

Time doesn't really go along from North to South or East to West, traveling like a storm through the sky. How come moments flow so smoothly; how come there is never a slip up, one of them bumping into another? In any kind of real system this would sometimes happen, wouldn't it?

Actually I don't think there is any time, really. I am time. That's what I actually am, and that's what time actually is, because if there wasn't anything there wouldn't be any time. And if there weren't anything I couldn't think about time and then certainly there would be no time; there's time because I think so, because there are words and because there are people who speak to one another. I'm sure someone has already said this somewhere in another way. I do of course read books although I often forget what they say.

Space is the place where everything that there is is, space is the out there to time's in here. No space no time, and no time no space. Someone has also already told about this I am sure.

No one has imagined that they can have time. We don't know what time is, but certainly you can't fool it or manipulate it or change it or own it. We may kid ourselves about this, but everyone really knows that they are time and that time goes along at its pace and then it runs out for us. We are gone and there is no more time. Everyone knows that and no one really tries to get around it.

But because people know they can't own time they try mightily to own space, to own place. History is the history of property. Since people can't have time they want space but it's hopeless. How can you own it? You go away but the place is still there. It's amazing.

It's as if you were trying to hold the ocean in your hand.

In Buddhism one of the precepts is non-possessiveness. We used to translate that precept "a disciple of the Buddha does not possess anything, not even the Truth." Knowing that you can't possibly possess anything is the Truth already. We know we have various stuff, but this only means we are the servant of that stuff, it is our responsibility to take care of it, to nurture it, to treat it with the greatest respect. This is pretty hard to do and do well. It's not a matter of being materialistic or not materialistic. Good Zen practitioners are really very materialistic. They can appreciate the things that are there, knowing how wonderful, how really amazing they are, time and space flowing endlessly by, we ourselves flowing endlessly by.

If all that's so, then how is it God gave the land (and if you believe the Israeli right wing — all of the land, every inch promised in the Bible) to the people. For thousands of years this fact meant the evocation of a sadness constant in human life, of loss, and of hope that always comes when there is loss that with each loss there is renewal, until gradually Zion became known deeply as a place in the human heart, a place that was not a place but the flow of time and space itself.

And yet the human heart in the human body is not no place it must be some place and so it is not so simple to be human. Martin Buber once wrote to Gandhi that God's granting of the land to the people does not mean that God gives "any portion of the earth away, so that the owner may say as God says in the Bible, 'For all the earth is Mine (Exodus 19:5)'. The conquered land is, in my opinion, only lent even to the conqueror who has settled on it — and God waits to see what he will make of it."

Maybe the Jews who insist on having the land, who insist on the impossible, do so not out of greed or hatred but because they can't stand the loss that they have sustained in the past, that they do sustain in the present with the daily passage of time.

TALK

SHABBAT. THIS IS THE TIME BEYOND TIME when the world ceases its movement and color and struggle and suddenly, with sundown, peace reigns. The Shabbat bride, who is time's fullness in the present moment, comes in as if for the first time, and everyone is thrilled, this is the word, thrilled to greet her. Since she is invisible everything stands for her.

And so we are anxious to get to the Kotel (the famous Western Wall, known everywhere else except here, in Jerusalem, as the Wailing Wall). The sun is drawing down, making shadows long, and the light is very pensive and rich as we arrive. There is an ever growing hubbub of people milling about in the courtyard, everyone full of happiness and anticipation. In the midst of the shifting crowd there seem to be ten or twelve different minyans, prayer groups, going on at once, each with a different costume and style of prayer. One large group of coatless young men, all wearing freshly starched white shirts and black trousers, are praying very loudly, joining hands to dance in a circle as they sing. There are several different Hasidic groups — one with large fur hats and cutaway coats belted at the waist, one with black suits and round black hats, one with gray lightweight cloth coats that look like bathrobes. Each group is its own world, decidedly separate from the other, and it's difficult for us to figure out where exactly we belong. Finally a young man approaches us and says, minyan, you know what it is? And when we say yes he leads us forward somehow among the ever thickening sea of bodies until suddenly somehow the sea seems to part and we are in the middle of a suddenly created minyan which is already, without any signal, beginning the prayers. This group is a modern orthodox group, all wearing the tiny knitted kipah fastened to the hair with pins — which in fact we ourselves are wearing. We seemed to have joined the fastest minyan on the block — no singing (except for a version of L'cha Dode, the song of welcoming the Sabbath Bride, which we don't know), no monkey business, one, two, three and the preliminary prayers for Shabbat are through. As we pray we have to press closer to the leader to hear where we are in the service amid the din of other groups singing chanting davening and shuckling, everywhere the ancient characteristic shuckling, the trance-like awkward and yet enormously graceful unselfconscious swaying, even the young boys bouncing back and forth like those weighted balloons that you hit and they immediately bounce back. Meanwhile the darkness gathers and the wall before us changes to a deeper brown. But we are so fast we have to pause to wait for full darkness without which the Shema can't be said. Finally it comes as swallows wheel and shriek overhead, and we conclude our prayers and the group disperses unceremoniously.

Here's our friend Gil the American Chasid who invited us to Shabbat dinner several days ago. He gathers us and a few more of his flock together — Edward, a USA college student in Israel on Ohlpahn, to study, and to see the world, and Michael a young hippie from Canada — and off we go to his nearby apartment. In addition to us also Gil's wife and small daughter, and an Iraqi woman of great enthusiasm and very confused English.

Dinner consists of a good soup, lots of wine, challah, a vegetarian lasagna, and conversation.

Gil's views are pretty straightforward and are aired didactically, with a view particularly to me, who ought to give up trying to be

Japanese, navel-gazing, and getting hung up on nothingness, and to Edward, who ought to give up his notion of wandering up and down trying out this and that and return to his roots. It's like this — if you ask me the way to your hotel I'll tell you turn left right right and left — if you insist on going this way, your own way, you may or may not get to your hotel but it will certainly take you a lot longer and you may get into trouble with Arabs along the way. So why not save yourself the trouble and pay attention to someone who already knows the way?

I'm not saying that the goyim are less than we are, but God created a world in which all things are different, each thing has its own place. Jews are Jews, goyim are goyim, and I respect the righteous goy. Look, take a pygmy — if he loses his family he can wander around in the bush without any landmarks because he has an inborn homing instinct — that's his nature. Watusis are good at basketball but pygmies are not. The Jew is born to use the intellect — to study Torah, that's our talent. Sure you can try something else, and since Jews are always good at whatever they do, you'll be good at it — maybe you'll even become a roshi — but you'll always come up against a wall — because you're a Jew — God made you a Jew for a purpose. And that's what you need to do.

The point is the Jews have got to keep the mitzvot, study Torah. Look at my hand — the fingers separate, each one different, but look! One hand! Everything's like that. So — you reap what you sow — and if a Jew doesn't keep the commandments it affects everyone, not just him. It's like the guy in the boat who's drilling a hole into the boat — guy next to him says hey cut that out! and he says, whaddya mean, I paid my ticket, this is my seat, I can do what I want! But he's going to sink the whole boat! So it's up to you — if you don't do it right you're going to drag the whole world down.

Why do you think the Holocaust happened? Do you think it was an accident? No! God said, hey come back home, the time is right. And what did we say? What! I go to that dirty country and be a farmer? I'm a big doctor here in Germany, I'm the professor,

I'm the important guy. So God says, OK, sure, you have free will, go ahead. But if you don't go home, I'm gonna give you. And boy did he give us.

But now that we're here we're not gonna leave — never! This is our land. Where are you from? Canada? You own a house? Do your parents? And where did they get it from? They bought it. And where'd the people they bought it from get it? So somebody grabbed it from the Indians — and the Indians grabbed it from the cavemen. But this piece of land is the only one in the world that has a deed and title — it's in the Bible — look it up. As a Jew you own a piece of this land — somewhere here there is a piece of land for you. So we're gonna give back some of the land? Who's gonna give back? What're they talking about?

So you want to go to India, to Nepal? I'll save you the trouble — listen, I've been through all that already — you don't have to do it. I was in India seven years — three and a half years I didn't talk, I just meditated twenty-three hours a day. I stood on one foot in the briar patch, whatever it was, where if you fall you're gonna get a thorn stuck in you, I did it all. And it wasn't a picnic: I was in a big pit, believe me, and all the stuff just got me in deeper — but God says when you sin and get into a pit if you turn that pit turns inside out it becomes a mountain and you're on top of the mountain — and I am, high and happy, Baruch Hashem! I was in Japan, I learned kanji, I was grinding the ink, meditating. You know in the Bible it says Abraham had several children; to Isaac he gave his inheritance — but the others got gifts. Gifts it says. This and that. So these other ways, they have gifts. In India the guru that I was with you could ask him for anything — what? — a diamond — whatever it was — and he'd wave his hand there would be a diamond. So that's what I got there — some powers — but in the end what did it amount to? Let me tell you about Jewish meditation — it's not blanking out or going to zero. No: Shema Yisrael Adonoy Elohenu...so then you think about that, what it means, all day long you go around pondering it, constantly thinking about it. That's the first way, then Shema....Echad....So

Echad, then quiet. Nothing. Just silence. So this is the nothing of
you Buddhists, see, but you don't get stuck there. No, you have to
put the two together, see. Now meditation has to do with the
intention behind what you do — so Shabbat is coming up. It's
Wednesday and I have to go to the market to shop for Shabbat,
and I have to run around like crazy to get ready, but all week long
I'm thinking about Shabbat — see Shabbat is zero, the six days are
like the contemplation — see how it works? So all week long is a
meditation. See — eat a big meal, drink wine, a little singing,
dancing, that's Jewish meditation. You don't need to fast, sit all
twisted up, cramp your legs. Just eat a piece of matzoh — God
makes it really easy for us...

Gil says all this with great eloquence, excitement and certainty,
pulling on his beard, waving his hands around, with a slightly
crazed look in his eye.

Gil's wife, when she hears I'm a Zen student says now that
she's heard it she can really see it — the short hair, the posture,
kind of complacent, centered. I say yes, and that she fits that
description too, and she does, a young woman, much younger
than Gil, as solid as he is effervescent.

I go into the bathroom — the toilet paper's already torn into
squares which are stacked on top of the toilet (you can't tear
toilet paper on Shabbat) — go in without benefit of light — you
can't turn on a light on Shabbat.

Rebuilding the temple — it's going to be really easy — it's
going to happen really quickly. Why? Because God's going to do
it. It just takes one more mitzvah and then the temple lowers
down from heaven, in fire, and that's it. The Meshiach comes
then and walks the city as king. Just one more mitzvah — it
might be just one more person I get to put on tfillin. The other
day a tour group comes and I ask the name of one guy —
someone tells me and I go up to him — he's standing near the
wall, and I say, hey Morris, God sent me to tell you to put on
tfillin. And boy he starts shaking and looking up to the sky — he
nearly plotzed. Sometimes I say, look come on over and put on

tfillin, just two more people and I'm gonna win a free trip to Miami. Believe me I work hard there, I yell, I scream, I fight. But I'm not kidding about the temple — it says this. Now there were two men, and one of them believes the Meshiach is gonna come in his time. And the other one says, nah, come on, no way. So they both die. So who's right? The one guy lived a happy, hopeful life. Everyday he was joyful because he woke up and it was gonna be today — the Meshiach is coming. The other guy was always disgusted — nothing good's gonna happen — just more trouble. So who was right and who was wrong?

After dinner Gil walks us down to the street to point out the way back to our hotel. At the bottom of the stairs, in the stone courtyard, another bearded Jewish man wearing a tallith, is standing talking to a few people in the warm dark Shabbat glow. As we pass by Gil remarks to him, sarcastically, under his breath, Hey you're looking religious tonight. The guy snarls back some kind of bitter response. In this momentary exchange I can see a whole relationship: Gil has been needling this guy for some time about the quality of his Jewish practice, he has done it with such relentless sarcasm that it has created hatred in him, it has made an enemy out of him. Whenever the guy sees Gil he sees red. Maybe this happened because Gil's a renegade, member of no particular sect, follower of no particular viewpoint, he has his own strong viewpoint that is completely in accord with the truth, and in stark contrast to other viewpoints which are flatly wrong. Maybe it's because he grew up as a reform Jew, with little education in Hebrew, he's self taught, which you can hear in his clumsy reading of the prayers, and so, as a member of the Jewish quarter community would hold low status, a position he refuses to acknowledge in any way. So he's a taunter, a critic, a spoiler, an outsider. He lives day by day, on donations, which makes the holding of his viewpoint and of his religious status not only an identity but also a livelihood, a very dangerous position indeed, one that probably doesn't promote humility nor tolerance.

On the way home in the dark through the quarter's winding

cobbled streets, some ancient, some newly reconstructed, Jeff and I talk about religious Zionism.

In the beginning Zionism and deep Jewish religiosity were mutually exclusive. The Zionists wanted a modern reaffirmation of Judaism based on the secular heroism of nineteenth century nationalism; the religious thought that was heresy: the entire rabbinical interpretation of the Torah had to do with exile. It was only by our religious acts, our acts of observance, that God would be moved to send the Messiah to bring about not only the return to the Holy Land, but also the transfiguration of the historical world. The Zionists saw this viewpoint as backward, and worse, as an invitation to the oppression that came from isolation and rejection of the modern world. The Holocaust of course changed the economy of this divergence in viewpoint. With the seemingly overnight discovery of the six million dead and the millions of refugee survivors suddenly cast out homeless all over Europe, it was obvious that only something absolutely new in Jewish history could redeem, could make sense of, the historical moment. And the Zionists exploited this fully. Once the state was created the religious parties had a symbolic and a legal function: they stamped the state with the Kosher "U," gave it an ancient poetic imagery, and they helped make a majority in the Knesset. But they were really irrelevant. After the '67 war, with the capture of all that territory, territory originally granted by God in the Bible, and with the simultaneous and inevitable tarnishing of the Socialist dream that twenty years of power effected, the religious parties suddenly woke up and discovered their real destiny: this victory ushered in the time of the Messiah — now politics, Biblical myth, and traditional observance were one, and there was a cause — the securing of all of the Holy Land for the chosen people. These were the settlers of Gush Emunim, fanatic, courageous, powerful, and they soon became the moral avant garde in Israel — until at least the beginning of the Palestinian uprising in late 1987.

This probably won't work out.

But the secular Zionist impulse has run out of answers.

History is truly beyond them now. Oddly enough, Jeff and I agree, what Israel needs now is some kind of religious viewpoint, one that takes into account a universal ethical imperative. And we agree: fanaticism is the enemy; secularism leaves too much out. But we both feel that any kind of balanced viewpoint gets lost in the din of the many strong voices always arguing. Everyone is caught in the passion of the debate. A voice that doesn't have something to protect does not shriek. And a voice that doesn't shriek isn't heard. To speak with some perspective, some sense of measure, seems oddly out of place, irrelevant. The Israeli will always take the high ground: what do you know, it's fine for you to say. There are real bullets in those guns. Israeli politics is reported in the papers and magazines all over the world as ordinary politics. But if there is an ordinary political event anywhere, it certainly did not take place in Israel. Politics in Israel begins and ends with the Holocaust, and this takes it out of the realm of ordinary discourse. The Holocaust was not an historical event. It was a black hole in history. It was a disease. The world has it and gave it to Hitler. He gave it to us and we haven't begun to find a cure. We don't even have an accurate diagnosis yet. And a politics based on such a disease, however much we can sympathize with it, is a politics that won't work. I don't mean that the Holocaust can be forgotten. Just because it is a black hole it is eternally a reference point. Human history, at least for a Jew, and therefore for a member of Western culture, can't be understood without it. And not only history: daily life can't be understood without it. But somehow we have got to digest it, incorporate it, move through it. This probably doesn't happen in forty or fifty years, or even in two or three generations.

Yes, well, at least we, Jeff and I, don't have to worry about it, we can go home and we can think about it a little and then forget it. And how do we feel about that?

When we get back to the hotel we tell Dad all about our dinner with Gil. But he's too excited and hyper to listen, full of his own ideas, telling jokes, kidding around, excited about our move tomorrow to Ashquelon, excited about seeing his long lost cousins, not particularly excited about being in Israel per se, because he seems a little bored or annoyed with traveling, but somehow experiencing some sort of release from whatever he was in the grip of earlier in the day, when he declined to come to the Kotel with us, preferring to stay home and rest. It's like the way he was when our mother died: suddenly cut loose from something that was tying him up in knots there was no way to untangle, even loosen up. That time we stayed up nearly all night together, the three of us, talking about everything until Jeff and I got tired and had to crawl off to bed, but Dad was still too excited to sleep and puttered around the apartment with this and that nearly till dawn.

This trip to Israel was supposed to have been for him and Mom. Now it was for us, not for him, to increase our Jewish spirit. And it was for the possibility of our children's inspiration as Jews. You couldn't explain it, he told us at breakfast. But it made sense. It doesn't really matter what I see or do here, he said. I've already seen and done more than I ever expected I would.

He's ready to go home.

ZENTATSU

THE FIRST TIME I SAW ZENTATSU was at a lecture he was delivering at the Zen Center in San Francisco. It was soon after the old Japanese abbot, Suzuki-roshi, died. Suzuki-roshi was loved by everyone. He was quiet, deep, and wise. Now here was his replacement, his successor, a tall young American, just back from several years in Japan, looking freshly shaven, all angular and bony, sharp in every way. All the Zen teachers I had ever seen before were round, and all their features softly turned inward, toward their bellies or toward the earth. But Zentatsu was sharp, and his features pointed out and up toward the sky. When he spoke it was as though he were figuring out what he was saying as he was saying it. As if he were in the process of adumbrating the shape of reality itself, which was ineffable although highly elaborate, and you participated with him in this as you listened. You didn't always understand what he was talking about but it was always fascinating and inspiring. After about ten years I could understand it pretty well.

He explained how Zen practice was the logical conclusion, the crowning touch, of Western science and history. How it was not only the answer to our personal problems, but the Answer to Everything: culture, politics, art. He was always very improvisational, very untraditional, very exciting in what he said. He had a marvelous way of drawing you in.

I didn't particularly take to him that first time. Afterward I got used to him and had a great deal of affection for him. Finally I came to love him, as I still do today, although it is a funny kind of love, like loving a rainstorm, or a rainbow, something inherently unreliable.

He was then and still is though in another way an extraordinary person, capable of doing many things at once, of living, like a corporate executive or head of state, at a very high and removed level of operation, on which webs of activity are set into motion below by casual words, thoughts, or gestures from above. He could give a brilliant talk, leap into his BMW, dictating a crucial fund raising letter en route, return home and pack while engaged in an important emotional phone call with a student, back in the car, onto the airplane, and land at a place where he would immediately proceed to a zendo where he would within moments be sunk in a deep transhuman trance state. That was more or less his life, day by day. I think he loved it. It stimulated and excited him.

At that time we were all convinced that being enlightened meant that a light bulb went off in your head and from that moment on everything you did was perfect and you could see right through everything. I wonder whether Zentatsu was convinced of that too. That's how it was: Zentatsu, hopelessly above and beyond the rest of us, setting the tone for all behavior and understanding, making all the decisions, taking care of everything. In a way it sounds crazy but it was all right. We had each other. We were doing something really wonderful none of us would ever have been able to do alone. We were also building a great institution that we believed would have an important effect on Western civilization. It was all probably true.

Zentatsu operated full bore day and night. Work, play, meditation, night life, travel, it was all one seamless flow. He liked to eat out at fancy restaurants, hang around with prominent people, especially people in the arts, go out dancing, buy expensive clothes, art and books. Whatever he needed he bought, no matter what it cost, and it was always the best thing you could get and often it was obscurely the best thing from a foreign country, a thing no one had heard of yet but would be hearing a lot about very soon. He explained all of this in terms of Zen, in terms of culture, in terms of social change. This was the way to influence people. This was the way to advance the cause of the Dharma, to help all beings. It wasn't a question of doing these things out of personal preference.

Later on when we found out that in addition to all these explanations it was also the case that Zentatsu really did have personal preferences even deep needs for all of these things we were really surprised. It seems foolish now that we were surprised then, and it is hard to explain why. Perhaps it was because we had high aspirations for our lives and had placed those aspirations in Zentatsu's hands. We wanted him to show us that life can be grander than the newspaper says it is. We knew it was so — and it is so — but we didn't have confidence enough in ourselves or in the teachings of the Buddha to make it so. So we were surprised. Everyone was surprised.

In many lectures Zentatsu used to say, trust yourself, trust yourself absolutely. This practice rang very true to me and so I took it to heart and tried to live my life that way. But it's pretty hard because the more I really tried to stake everything on myself the more I could see myself about as solid as smoke, and the more confused I got. If I tried to trust my opinions absolutely I could see how much they shifted day to day, based on what I was reading or who I was talking to or what my experience lately had been. If I tried to trust my basic ideas about who I was I could immediately see that these were just ideas, they could not support the weight of my whole trust, they were too flimsy. So I was pretty mixed up. Then it dawned on me that I had been misunderstanding the message: it was not to trust myself as self, but to trust my experience as it arose. And my experience consisted not only of what was inside my head, but also of many other things.

When I saw clouds, clouds were my experience. When I heard a bird, the song was my experience. When someone told me what a jerk I was, that was my experience, not something coming from someplace else, to be defined out and defended against. So in this way I worked very hard at trusting my experience absolutely, even my mixed up thinking, right to the end, staying with it, not glancing off, and finally I could find always at the end of my experience, whether I liked the experience or not, a sky-like mind, in which every experience was very broad and deep.

And that's the way I trusted Zentatsu. Not as some other guy, but as my own experience. And in that way I could use him to understand and deepen my life, which worked out all right, more or less.

So the more I discovered he could be wrong, could be stupid about things, the more I liked him. Rather than being discouraged by his weaknesses I was cheered up by them, spurred on to more effort in my own practice. I remember once we were preparing a big important ceremony, very complicated, and as complicated as these things can be, Zentatsu always had a way of making them more complicated or at least making them seem more complicated, which made them more exciting and dangerous. I think he enjoyed it very much when life was complicated and dangerous and hated it when it wasn't. Anyway, I was in charge of preparing the ceremony, it was almost time to begin, and Zentatsu came into the zendo to check things out. It was just the moment when he needed to be most intense, most concentrated on the ceremony, but instead he seemed very nervous, very distracted, a little confused and angry. Instead of wearing his robes he was wearing some kind of bright casual clothing. And behind him, at the door of the zendo, was a very beautiful woman, a student, also dressed casually, waiting for him. I looked at him, I looked at her, I looked at the zendo all in a flurry of worrisome religious activity and I thought it was marvelous. Here we were about to plunge into a ceremony that, if it worked, was going to put us right into the middle of the heart of the mystery of life, and here he was, so hopelessly in love he couldn't even think about it. Isn't that just how life always is?

It was his brief affair with this student (both Zentatsu and the student were married) that mixed us all up in the spring of 1983 and led to Zentatsu's resignation. It wasn't really so bad I think that there was such an affair. Bad, but not that bad.

But the incident blew the lid off the pot. And all the things that had been simmering inside for a long time suddenly boiled over. Everyone had been thinking all along, I'd better not think about all this stuff I'm concerned about for my own life because I need to give up all that for the Dharma, and we did, we did stop thinking about it. But it kept on simmering in there unknown to us. Now it all came spurting out and everyone got pretty angry about all the sacrifices they had made. It's all right of course to make sacrifices and to give up what you want personally for a greater good. It's a fine thing to do and it gives you a sense of great purpose. But you have to do it with clarity, without putting lids on pots while the heat is still on. You need to keep abreast of what you are actually thinking underneath.

And the worst part was that everyone had this creepy feeling when the lid came off, almost a psychotic feeling.

When I was a boy I remember eating breakfast while my mother watched me. Every now and then I'd come upon a blackened Cheerio in the cereal bowl and I would imagine that this was a poisonous Cheerio and that I would die when I ate it and that the woman watching me eat it though she looked exactly like my mother was not my mother at all but had killed my mother and was posing as her and was now killing me. I ate the blackened Cheerio very slowly and with the most horrid feeling that the world was evil and upside down. I think this is a common experience for children.

Well, something like that happened to all the students in the Zen Center. Suddenly our trusted teacher although he looked the same turned into someone else someone evil and suddenly the many events of the last twelve years were reevaluated reinterpreted and events that we never did know about or knew about in a way but hadn't noticed much became very noticeable. And when you have hundreds of people feeling these things and getting one another all wound up about them you have a really mixed up and very painful situation.

And the worst part was that Zentatsu got defensive and he got confused. Everyone wanted him to cry and go into shock go into retreat do penance suffer and apologize, but instead he kept running around, running away, admitting his failings but not admitting them at the same time. And the logs of his defensiveness and running away got thrown right onto the fire, giving it more and more crazy energy.

What everyone wanted in the weeks and months that followed was an explanation for all this. And there were a lot of explanations. There were many portraits drawn of the community and, of course, many drawn of Zentatsu. That he was a sociopath, that he fundamentally lacked an understanding of the Dharma, that his personality disorders were such as to make it impossible for him really, ever, to have healthy relationships with students unless he sought professional help and worked his way out of it. Everyone acknowledged his brilliance but thought maybe the brilliance itself had created the barrier.

But the one of course who sought longest and deepest for explanations was Zentatsu himself. He had always been the master of explanation and now he had found a problem that almost defied him. His brain was working time and a half trying to understand. I remember once seeing him standing staring out the window of a restaurant at the parking lot outside, after a long conversation we'd had about it all, looking thoroughly exhausted, distracted and confused. It was very sad. I had never seen him look quite that way before. I remember another time, a long evening during which we discussed and discussed and discussed it all, but didn't really discuss, actually I followed him down elaborate passageways through darkened corridors, into doorways and up steps into attics and down steps into basements hallways living rooms of explanations until my head spun going with him step by step until truly I didn't know anything anymore about anything.

I am writing these words in late 1989, almost seven years since the events occurred. For these seven years we have been trying to find a way to make peace, to have friendship, because it is really sad not to have it. There have been lots of incidents in those seven years, mostly bad, a very few slightly good, but we are still very far away from making friends. This is because within the universe of the explanations of the Zen Center there is no place for the explanations of Zentatsu; and even more so within the universe of the explanations of Zentatsu there is no corner for the explanations of the Zen Center.

Now it is 1994, nearly 1995, and there is still no real resolution for all of this. More or less things have normalized. I see Zentatsu seldom, when I do I am glad to see him, but I know there is still a lot of sadness.

This is too bad but it's not that bad. No one is harming anyone, and I am especially happy that the Zen Center has not, on the few occasions when Zentatsu has done difficult things, reciprocated with difficult things.

In the end I think everyone needs an explanation for his or her life and everyone needs to affirm that explanation mightily. But I think he also needs to see that lots of other explanations are true also. It says somewhere in Zen literature, "Everything is true, everything is false."

Reconciliation, which is after all, the main point of Zen practice, to freely move in, not to get caught in, the opposing forces in our life, means to embrace the other guy's story, to embrace your own story, to embrace all stories, and have the nerve to act on that. There's a great risk involved.

In the end I think peace may be more dangerous than war.

G'NAT SHOMRON

A FEW DAYS AGO WE WENT OUT TO DINNER with Moishe and Panina in Jerusalem. It was a good meal. Israeli vegetarian, in a crowded New Age type of place. We discussed at length social conditions in Israel. Israelis pay high taxes; although Moishe's salary is somewhat less than ten thousand dollars he is in the highest tax bracket, about fifty percent. Worker production is low because all male workers under the age of fifty-five take forty days off a year (not counting vacation) to go to the army for reserve duty. Husbands take no tax deductions for a wife and children; only the women can take deductions for children. On the other hand, hospital costs of child bearing are all free, and you receive from the state automatically cash deposited in a bank account for the child when it is born, and you continue to receive monthly cash payments until the child is grown. With each additional child you receive higher payments. With four children Moishe and Panina receive the equivalent of over four hundred dollars a month for their children. Raising children is thus encouraged, and in fact taking care of and cherishing mothers and children seems to be a conscious and sacred purpose of the state of Israel. On the kibbutz, Michelle explained that after six weeks the child is given up to the children's house where he stays all day till four o'clock. Since the mothers are only required to work half a day they get the afternoons to rest — no work, and no children. Statistics show that these kibbutz-raised children grow up strong and healthy — at least they have in the past. It may be different now. A high percentage of army officers are kibbutzniks. Even outside the kibbutz there is free state-sponsored childcare all day after the age of two. Women are thus encouraged both to have children and to work. In Israel there are banks everywhere. In the banks you do all your financial business — pay all your bills, investments, etc. Loans are hard to get. To buy a house you have to put eighty percent of purchase price down. Since prices are high one must have quite a bit of money to buy an apartment — and all over Israel everyone says they don't know how anyone does this, salaries being so low, and they also say — but we manage! It is apparently a kind of financial miracle that can only happen in the Holy Land (although the fact that there is now a custom that the parents contribute to buy an apartment for newlyweds helps). Because of galloping inflation, which is now, baruch hashem ("blessed be the name of God"), under control, it was possible to, say, as happened to Moishe and Panina, to lose one's life savings virtually overnight. An account they had started for their son disappeared within a few years this way — it became so little money that the bank wanted to close it out. Panina and Moishe constantly expressed, oddly with a great deal of enthusiasm and joy, the frustration, the difficulties, even the social lunacies, of living in Israel — they are very happy here and do not at all mind these problems. In the states, they say, life is fairly routine and in Israel every day you live and die with the news — things happen, the government does things, that really affect the individual. Every day there is some controversy, some life and death crisis. You learn to live with this, they say. In return, you get a deep sense of purpose, a sense of mission. Life may not be easy, but you know why you are alive.

At breakfast next morning Dad is very agitated as he speaks about his friend Morris Ryant. Morris is always popping angina pills. Of course he does have a heart condition, but, Jesus, he goes too far. He's so damned nervous about it all of the time that it's a pain in the ass for all his friends because we are constantly hearing about Morris' angina pains which appear in the damnedest places. Now I asked my doctor about this because I get these angina pains over here in the heart area or sometimes in the shoulder and I said is that where you get them and the doctor says yes of course that's where you get them. But Morris claims he has them all over — in his arms, in his neck, in his head, even his balls! — everywhere! And constantly! I swear to God he must be immune to the angina pills he's taking — so many, or he owns stock in the company! He even gives himself a shot of morphine when it gets really bad. Of course when I get it also it's bad. It scares hell out of me. What time is the bus?

We take the bus from our hotel in Jerusalem down to Ashquelon.

Going down from Jerusalem to the South and then turning West, toward the coast — in this forested region we pass marker after marker of war graves and battle sites in the woods beside the road. Moving toward the sea we are in the coastal plains, passing much agricultural land (here you see irrigation pipes and wide green fields, and mile after mile of orange groves). By 11 A.M. we are in Ashquelon. Simon and Hilda pick us up and we drive to a park where we view antiquities and sit on a hill overlooking the Mediterranean which is a deep blue-green, with a curious purplish color where the darker blue water at the horizon meets the dark sky. The light is bright and the day is lovely. Simon tells me how he came to the states from Ruskova, a town now in Romania, though at one time in the Austro-Hungarian empire, and then between the wars part of Hungary. During the war everyone was deported — the very young and the old, anyone who could not work, went to death camps, the others to forced labor camps. That's where he went and thus survived though many of his family — three of his nine brothers and sisters as well as his parents — perished in the camps. When he speaks of this, mentioning the names of his relatives who were killed, he cannot complete the sentence saying what happened to them; instead he ends in mid-sentence with a characteristic sigh. After the war he went to a displaced persons camp, then emigrated to the USA, where he met his wife Hilda, who was his second cousin and whose family he had therefore known in Ruskova. He was only about twenty years old, had no trade (he had only studied in the Yeshiva at Ruskova and had never worked), had an uncle in New York who was a butcher, so he became a butcher — a trade he practiced for over thirty years before retiring in 1981. Did he like it? No, not at all. Why not? He didn't like the heavy work, he was not made to lift and carry. Thank God he has had good health but he was not made to do this kind of work. His father and mother, separately, had also emigrated to the States about the time my grandfather, my father's father, had, before W.W.I, but Simon's mother and father returned. Why? America was too goyishe for them — so they returned to Ruskova where they could live thoroughly as Jews, at least until doing so proved fatal to them. Simon and Hilda, Europe in ruins, did not possess this luxury or choice, and they stayed in America, goyishe or not, but one by one their children, who inherited a passion for religious observance from their grandparents, found no other way but to make aliyah to Israel, and once all the children were gone, Simon and Hilda followed.

We drive around Ashquelon. It's a town that at once reminds me of coastal California — bright sun, bright sea, shining architecture — and of the town in Pennsylvania where I grew up — the older streets near the center of town looking quite run-down. Eliezer, Simon and Hilda's brother-in-law, runs a small candy-liquor-everything store on the main street that looks like an American store of fifty years ago — dark inside, little lots of individual candies displayed in glass cases, plain wooden shelves with a motley range of merchandise. Across the street from his store is a new modern department store. The town seems quiet and a little unkempt. People dress plainly and not much English is spoken. Open lots in odd places full of tall weeds.

Here we stop at a modest apartment development to visit Bela and Eliezer. Pearl, another sister of Simon's, is also here. So Dad is meeting these three first cousins, Holocaust survivors, for the first time. We are greeted in Yiddish with tremendous enthusiasm, ushered into a modest dining room and given sweet liquor and honey cakes. Tremendous talking in Yiddish, all at once, about names apparently, who everyone is named after. Simon's parents, killed in Auschwitz, were named Moishe and Devorah, and there are consequently in the family several Moishes and Devorahs. Also discussed is the Yiddish language, and various foods of the old country. In Ruskova surnames weren't used — though many people had the same names they were distinguished from another by always using the father's name: Simon's Moishe is different from Eliezer's Moishe, and so on. Only the postmaster or the government official knew from surnames. Bela, Eliezer, and Pearl (who is childless and whose husband died many years ago) are, like the rest of the family, thick, short people, plump but sturdy. Their faces are faces of the Eastern European peasantry and their gestures and manner of speaking are also Eastern European. They seem to be happy, simple people, enjoy family (they pull out picture albums, talk about their children, and ask us about ours), food, think about money and business. If you work you have money but no time, if you don't work you have time but no money, is a saying of Eliezer's, who has just sold his little candy business.

After the liquor, which is drunk with a very moving toast, the meal begins — delicious chopped liver, chicken soup, stuffed cabbage and chicken, cake for dessert — a really wonderful Old World meal which is eaten heartily with much voluble conversation. Everyone takes a family snapshot. Dad's really thrilled to be speaking Yiddish, surprised he can do it so well, pleased to be understood, pleased to meet so many cousins he didn't know he had, and to be hearing about life in the country his father came from.

On our way from Ashquelon to G'nat Shomron ("Shomron" means "Samaria," the Biblical name for what is otherwise known as "West Bank"), where Simon and Hilda live, we drive through Kefar Sava, where they used to live, and drive past their old house. When they first moved to Israel they spent several months living in an absorption camp in Tel Aviv while this house was being built, going back and forth in Moishe's station wagon to "supervise" construction. We pull into the pleasant dead end street lined with stuccoed, tile-roofed houses (It's so much built up now, Hilda remarks proudly, when we built here only four years ago all this was trees and vacant lots — you can't believe how fast they are building this country up) and the across-the-street neighbor rushes out to greet them, Hilda leaping out of the car and conversing at great length in Hebrew with this woman who is a professor of Holocaust studies at nearby Bar Ilion University where Devorah, Hilda's daughter, went years ago for a year's study. It was this trip of Devorah's that led ultimately first to her, and then to the whole family's, aliah.

The husband also comes out — he's principal of the local school — hugs, kisses, and has to run, pulls his car out of the driveway, nearly running into Simon's car as he tries to get out of the driveway, a complicated jockeying of cars ensues, he goes on, and out runs the down-the-street neighbor, Hilda leaps out, and they converse at length in English, this woman's British, overwhelmingly friendly and good-humored, she's a music teacher and in the middle of a lesson so has to say good-bye and greetings to the whole mishpucha (this after a ten-minute conversation) and on the way out we run into still another neighbor who gives kisses and greetings (she speaks English with a European accent) and says everyone, Baruch Hashem, is well.

Driving on we go through a few Arab villages, notably Qalqilya, which has lately been in the news because it is here that this week some Arabs have thrown Molotov cocktails into Israeli cars — one, a week or so ago, landed in someone's car and blew it up. The tension may have begun, according to Devorah, when an IDF soldier forbade Arabs from working the fields near Qalqilya (this has always been Arab territory but now is occupied) and the Arab went home and told people the Israelis had attacked his wife. Then a mass of Arab men returned with rocks and confronted the Israeli soldier, who, in panic perhaps, fired into the air and into the ground (Israeli soldiers are forbidden to fire at anyone unless their life is being directly threatened — in the news today there is a man being court-martialed for violating this rule) and finally the crowd disbursed. Then came the Molotov cocktail throwing. Apparently done by a twelve-year-old boy who was caught. A curfew on the town was lifted yesterday. But we roll up our windows as we drive through the street lined with various Arab shops, men sitting in the doorways as we pass. Gush Emunim, the militant settlers' organization, is apparently not satisfied with the response of the IDF to this affair (as we drive through it is a great relief somehow to see the soldiers with their machine guns patrolling the streets. I am surprised at my feeling this way since in the United States the sight of an armed policeman or an armed soldier — this latter a rare sight — seldom makes me feel secure, rather makes me feel nervous, as though I might be picked up for something. But here it is the Arabs that make me feel nervous, I feel a little on edge in the Arab quarter in Jerusalem, and now a little nervous driving through Qalqilya) and they are organizing vigilante parties to patrol the village and are actively intimidating the Arabs. Rabin in the papers has been calling Gush Emunim's action a "pogrom" and in a discussion last evening Devorah is angry that Rabin says this — when the Arabs throw Molotov cocktails this is all right but whatever the Gush Emunim do is a pogrom. To be sure not all the Arabs are terrorists. Although they may not like the Jews moving in here to these hilltop settlements of expensive new homes (which are in effect, as Roi pointed out to us, subsidized by the government in this way — since the land is occupied territory, which is not officially part of the state of Israel, it can't be privately held. The government owns it and will lease it for forty-nine years to a settler, to be renewed for another forty-nine years, for one shekel. In other words, the land is free, you pay for house) at least the Jews bring an economic benefit to the Arabs — Qalqilya is booming, many of the Arabs are now able to build decent homes, the stores are busy (Jews shop here quite a bit) and all the construction work on the settlement is done by local Arabs. However, if the Qalqilya Arabs prove unfriendly or otherwise uncooperative then Arabs from somewhere else in the territories will be hired and shopping will be done at some other grocery store. In the end I think this is the biggest problem for the Jewish state. It is not so much a matter of territory as one of class. How can a state exist if all its citizens are lawyers, doctors, dentists, and professors? Who will do the manual work? The Palestinians in the territories will do it because there are no other opportunities. They are not citizens, and despite Israeli arguments that they are better treated than the vanquished have been or are elsewhere in the world, they have no rights and no real possibilities. For them the West Bank is not so much some land. It represents a chance, an identity. Nor is it land for Israel. For them it is security and it is also identity. For the Palestinians it means getting what they've never had and in truth will never get from the land itself. For the Israelis it means protecting what they have and can only lose with the holding of this land. For Simon and Hilda and Moishe and Panina it is, simply, a good place to live.

Finally we arrive here at G'nat Shomron, another West Bank hilltop settlement. The place all spanking new, construction going on everywhere, big boulders dug out of the hillside lying around here and there, the sidewalks not even in yet and, as at all the other settlements, the streets full of kids, here, since this is a religious settlement, all of the boys wearing kipot.

Hilda and Simon are proud of their house and to be sure it is the equal of an American suburban house and more — pseudo-marble floors in the kitchen, bathrooms upstairs and down, huge refrigerator, two entire dishwashing and food preparation areas (milk and meat), patio, picture windows. The same formica and plastic materials that you see in the States. Devorah's house, which we see the next day, is even bigger, five bedrooms, with a

107

finished basement below that is larger than the trailer we live in at Green Gulch by about three or four times. From Devorah's back terrace you can look out onto the front door of Hilda's house seen in between two other houses.

SESSHIN

SESSHIN IS A TRADITIONAL PRACTICE OF ZEN; the word means "gathering the mind." A sesshin lasts usually seven days, and during that time we sit on our cushions meditating all day long, even during meals, beginning early in the morning and into the night. The purpose of sesshin is not to take a rest but to try to see more clearly what your life actually is. Most of the time things are pretty busy, pretty complex, and it's hard to consider what's really important in your life. During sesshin there's nothing else to do. The difficulty of sitting there all that time is sufficient to raise up in the mind questions that you perhaps don't even particularly want to think about. And then to continue with the meditation you have to deal with these questions at a level deeper than thought, because if you just think about them it's hard to sit there, and you soon exhaust thought's resources. By the end, everyone who does sesshin feels purified, clean, as if the eyes, the whole body and mind, had been washed off very thoroughly. Usually the day after sesshin is a marvelous, light-hearted, wonderful day of no cares or worries.

Once during a break in sesshin I was standing on the roof of our Zen Center building in San Francisco looking down at the street. Cars were going by. Then I saw Neurit and her son Erez come to cross the street. Neurit is an Israeli woman who came to practice at Zen Center some years ago. Several Israelis have come over the years and they usually have a hard time. They are looking for something, some way out of an impossible situation, but it seems they can't wholeheartedly wish for that way out, so usually they can only go so far with the practice. Most of them practice for a while and then move on. You see them around the Bay Area here and there, and sometimes they come back once in a while. Neurit is like that. She lives near the Zen Center. Watching her and Erez cross the street was really marvelous. Neurit is a large, confident and impressive woman. She just marched across the street, without looking particularly to see if any cars were coming, marched across like the queen of the street, regal and dignified. Erez was ten steps behind her, following her. Cars were getting confused, stopping suddenly in the intersection, honking their horns. They couldn't see Erez very well, he's only five. When Neurit noticed this she turned around and raised her hands motioning the cars to stop, a little indignant, not at all non-plused, until Erez could get across the street. Then, without looking back, she and Erez went on.

Varda, another Israeli woman, was participating in the sesshin. She was on the serving crew. She was very impressive, walking into the meditation hall with the various pots of food, also very dignified, concentrated, and confident.

When I was a boy I didn't like the image of European Jews all bent over, oblivious, fatalistic, narrow, intellectual, neurotic, nervous, as it seemed to me. I didn't like the posture, the attitude that was presented to me as a model for how I was supposed to be. That's why I had an immediate and intuitive attraction to the Israeli ideal which was consciously quite different. I remember reading in school about the "Sabras," the Israeli-born youth like the sabra, a fruit that was tough on the outside, soft on the inside. This great image of the nation-building, pioneering Jew who was energetic, capable, able to fix plumbing as well as read Torah. From an early age I identified with that image. It was a matter of going beyond, of being liberated, from the past. These were Jews who were the opposite of my parents. My parents communicated to me in a thousand little ways every day that very little was possible, that in the end nothing was going to work out, but if you protected yourself and didn't try for too much you could squeak by unnoticed. But these Israeli Jews seemed to embody the opposite view: that anything is possible, that we can make anything work, we can start a new nation, build it from nothing, protect it, make the deserts bloom and the seas yield their harvests, and we can survive, no matter how many millions oppose us.

Neurit met and married Gerhardt, a German, at the Zen Center. They are divorced now. Gerhardt lived for many years at the Zen Center. He had tremendous personal problems and there seemed to be no end to his difficulties, and there seemed to be no way for him to get hold of it, to change things in his life no matter how hard he tried; he himself, and the world around him as it impacted him every day, seemed organized for nothing but tough times.

There are other people like this in the Zen Center who have a great deal of suffering in their lives and can't seem to shake it. I often talk to them and I have a great affinity with them because I can see myself that way too. The most rewarding time in practicing with people, for me, is when over the course of time people like that who have such a hard time, can begin to see some point, some worth in their lives, and begin to change. When a person who's had such a hard time begins even a little bit to be all right it's a tremendous thing. They usually have so much deep soulful wisdom underneath their pain. They usually are quite inspiring. They can remind you that even though there is a pit of suffering a hundred miles deep, like a well with completely smooth sides and no way to get out, still you can get out by just staying in, accepting the condition radically, and therefore transforming it, using it to advantage. The key seems to be seeing, really admitting, what the situation actually is. Not trying unrealistically to change things. In a way it's a matter of seeing how thoroughly impossible the situation is. This seems to be the beginning of change. In this way, there's always a glimmer of hope.

Avi and Shlomit are another couple of Israelis who practiced for a while at Zen Center. One day during a sesshin at Green Gulch I met them in the parking lot as I was walking through to go to my house on a break. They had come with an uncle of Avi's, a tough old kibbutznik. They wanted to show him around, to explain a little about Zen Center to him. I was glad to see them and stopped to talk for a minute. I told the uncle all about Green Gulch. He was most interested in our economy and the rules for our living together, how people came and went. Then I began speaking in grave terms about the situation in Israel, how impossible it seemed, how war seemed that it would go on and on. He was a jolly wily fellow, old and plump but sturdy-looking, and he laughed at my seriousness. He said, All over the world, if you look deeply, the prospects are only for peace. If you look at the details too much it seems impossible, but if you stand back and see it with a long view, the prospects are all for peace. He seemed to be speaking, at the end of a long life of struggle and sweat, about something he had seen, had seen intimately and certainly. I believed him.

A few weeks ago I went again to sesshin at our temple in San Francisco. I usually have a marvelous time at sesshin there. I am given a small room and all I have to do is wake up early in the morning and sit on my seat all day and eat meals and wash myself and sometimes I talk with some of the students about what is going on in their practice. During the breaks I look out the window or take a nap or clean my room or repair my robes. At this sesshin I had a roommate, my friend Lee de Barros, who is also a Zen priest. Lee is about fifty-five years old. He walks with a strange gait because he had polio when he was a boy and one of his legs is skinnier than the other and doesn't work quite right. He began Zen practice late in life. Before that he was a school-teacher and a social worker. He loves to help people the best he

can, that is what gives him the greatest pleasure. We are not supposed to talk during the breaks in sesshin but on one break Lee
said to me, while I was sitting at the table sewing, I have a theory
about evil. What is it? I said. Well, he said, the world is full of
people and all of them are different. Each of us only sees how we
are but we can't understand how other people are. So when other
people do things out of their differentness we don't understand
it. So we impute motives or images onto them: they're bad or
they're out to get me, we think. Then we act on those imputa-
tions and images and, receiving this, they don't understand the
way we are acting and they impute motives and images onto us,
only now they have more of a reason to do this since we actually
have done something to them. And then we turn around again
and do the same to them again. And this is how it goes. Finally
there really is something called evil. And it comes from this kind
of misunderstanding.

I thought this was a very wise theory.

That sesshin ended with an important initiation ceremony.
One of the students receiving initiation was a young Israeli
woman named Liat. Small, lively, very intelligent, with large eyes
and a constant wry smile on her lips, Liat had only been at Zen
Center for a few months and would be going home in a few
weeks. She came to talk with me. I am afraid about going back,
she said. A few months ago in Montreal I was arguing vehement-
ly for Zionism and I was really willing to die for it. But now I
don't know. It seems as if there are two realities, a reality of non-
possessiveness that we study here, and a reality of deep possessiveness, that we have in Israel. I'm full of anxiety about going back
because I know that this won't make any sense in Israel and what
will happen to me? Will I be able to keep up my practice, will it
make any sense to me there? In two weeks when I return I'll be
on reserve duty. I'll be patrolling the border with Jordan probably. How am I going to do that?

There aren't two realities, I told her. There are endless realities, or none, or only one. Don't worry about going back. Just go

and when you are there embrace whatever is right about your life there. What you've experienced here can't be possessed any more than the West Bank can be possessed. She thanked me for the help I had given her with her practice. You don't need to thank me, I said. It was for myself. For you, but also for myself. I have a dream, I told her, that somehow Dharma can help in Israel. But how, she said, when Dharma is the opposite of what Israel is. I don't know how, I said. It's a dream I have.

Later on, just before the initiation ceremony, she pulled me aside in the hallway and whispered to me, Will I still be Jewish even though I am doing this ceremony? I don't know, I said. Am I still Jewish? Who knows? Who decides? There must be a bill about it in the Knesset.

This sesshin ended on December 8, the day celebrated as the day when Buddha achieved enlightenment. We had a big ceremony to commemorate that and I played the big drum for the ceremony. The drum stands outside the ceremony hall and as I stood out there waiting for my cue I noticed for the first time that there was a mezuzah on the doorpost leading into the hall. I knew that our building had been a residence hall for single Jewish women years ago, before we bought it, but I had never noticed before that there was a mezuzah on the doorpost.

KOL SHOFAR

I T'S SATURDAY MORNING and I am praying at Kol Shofar synagogue in Tiburon, Marin County, California. The melodies of the
prayers are very beautiful, some of them I remember from my
boyhood and some of them I seem to remember from some
other time. I really love to sing these melodies and say these
words, and when I do it I put my whole heart and soul into it. I
probably sing as loudly as deeply and with as much joy in the
singing as anyone else in the room, maybe more. I really feel as I
am singing that I'm in contact with God and with all the Jewish
people from the beginning who have said and sang these things. I
don't think about it like that. But I feel that way — full of a sense
of well being, a sense of belonging. As is the case in most small
synagogues I've been to, the weekly Shabbat services are held in a
small chapel. The main sanctuary is used only for big occasions —
holidays or Saturdays when there's a Bar Mitzvah. The rest of the
time there aren't enough people to fill it up, so we pray in the
little chapel. I feel more comfortable here anyway. We sit on
metal chairs facing the portable ark. There's a big bulletin board
on the wall behind the ark and below that a wide window which
looks out onto a hillside full of trees and bushes. It's raining hard
outside.

I began coming to Kol Shofar after my mother died to say Kaddish, the prayer that is said every day for eleven months after the death of a parent, spouse, or sibling. I always say, "I promised my mother I'd say Kaddish for her" but actually my mother didn't care about that because she never considered or thought about death, and even if she had, I don't think she'd've minded one way or another about Kaddish. Actually I promised myself. Actually I don't think I promised myself either. It was just clear that I was going to do it. I hadn't been to a synagogue in many years. So I looked in the phonebook for the nearest synagogue and it happened to be Kol Shofar.

Now I am standing and singing as they open up the ark. This is a great moment. The ark is open, you can see, you can feel the presence of the Torah, and everyone sings about "The Tree of Life" in appreciation of this marvelous book — but it doesn't make sense to call it a "book" — this marvelous lore, this record of a way of life, a heritage, that has been so powerful. You can feel it. I'm called up to the Torah. I'm really amazed that I can be called up to the Torah. It makes me really happy to be able to go up there, sing the blessing, and to have a portion read for me. Every week a portion is read and in that way, in a year's cycle, the whole Torah is read, and every year, at this time of year, this portion is read, and it is the story of what is happening in our lives at this time of year. When you really immerse yourself in the life of Torah that's how it is. It's uncanny but it's true.

David White is the rabbi at Kol Shofar. A handsome man, bearded with black hair, about my age, probably a few years younger, he's very enthusiastic and friendly, very religious and very committed. I like to listen to his sermons. He speaks without any pomposity or pedantry. He tells how he feels about the portion we are reading, and he tries to tie it in with the life we are actually leading, on a personal level, and sometimes with what is going on in the news. Sometimes when he talks people will interrupt him to ask questions. It's a small, intimate group, and you feel that people know each other well and actually care about what they are asking about. And David responds with humility and care. His point of view is always that we are Jews and we have our way of life. That is the way of life for us, an ethical way, with a big responsibility to try to change the mixed up world for the better. Our way is definitely the best for us. But other people have other ways that are good for them.

Once I made an appointment to see David and I told him that I was a Zen priest and how I felt about being Jewish. He was pretty amazed at how it all worked out. He seemed to understand, and we had a good shop talk about how religion is. He said that it was meditation that, years before, had awakened him to the spiritual power of Judaism. Before that he had gone to rabbinical school mostly to please his father, who was a rabbi, with no intention of practicing as a rabbi. But now, inspired, he truly has boundless enthusiasm and energy for the religious life. When he sings the prayers he closes his eyes and belts them out from the gut. He has a way of tilting his head to one side and leaning it back when he sings, a gesture that makes him look all the more ardent, almost painfully immersed in his love of God.

I have another friend, Alan Lew, who is a rabbi. He too was inspired toward that by meditation practice. Alan and I went to school together at the Writer's Workshop at the University of Iowa a long time ago. At that time he was young, married with a child, and had just dropped out of law school in order to pursue a career as a writer. We became very close. We were like two little boats bouncing up and down often with a great deal of violence in the great waves and storms of the 1960s. The times of these last twenty or thirty years really do seem like waves to me, going out and coming in, washing things away, bringing things that have been washed away and broken up back in again, turning everything upside down, agitating everything, and there has been little time of calmness in which to make sense of any of it.

After writing school both of us moved to California. Easterners, we looked at California then, as we did it, with no jobs or plans, or notions of what we would do, as a decisive courageous and reckless life gesture, like leaping off a cliff with our eyes closed, or jumping into an endless ocean with no thought of destination. And it felt like that to us for a number of years. Recently, on a trip with my family, I drove through the places where we first lived in California, many years ago, by the ocean. And they still do feel that way. It was a very strange feeling, to be seeing those places again, the same and yet different. To be in the present time and yet to be suddenly immersed exactly in the past. And now, as I write this, looking at the great blue layers of mountains beyond the city of Vancouver, I feel that these mountains themselves are the shape of time, of the past, present, and especially the future. I can't really explain what I mean. If I could I suppose there would be no need for me to continue writing.

Alan began Zen practice a few years after I did. He was always involved, as so many of us were then, with spiritual practice. He tried various things and I think eventually took up Zen because I was doing it. Not that he was in the habit of following my lead in things. Rather it was just there and a natural thing, finally, to do. We practiced together very closely for a number of years, both of us young, and in a very exciting time of our lives during an exciting period in an exciting place. I can't even remember anymore what happened then or what our life was like. But it was a wonderful time. We went to Tassajara monastery together. By then Alan was divorced and I had just married. So the three of us, Alan, Kathie and I, drove to Tassajara together to enter the training period. We got drunk along the way and got there late, lurching down along the mountain road in our old car full of stuff.

After a while Alan left the monastery and we stayed on. He met and fell in love with Sherril. Since Sherril was not a Zen practitioner, when it came time for them to marry they didn't feel right about a Zen wedding. So since they both happened to be Jewish they had a Jewish wedding. The rabbi whom they found to do it, Rabbi Abrami, was a Frenchman, I remember a very wacky but lovable man, quite disorganized and religious, with a slightly New Age touch. Soon Alan was throwing his not inconsiderable spiritual and intellectual energies into the practice of Judaism. Next, when Rabbi Abrami returned to France, Alan was acting as the informal leader of the congregation. And then, after a flood of letters from the congregation to the Jewish Theological Seminary in New York, he was a student there, a brilliant one, and now he is a rabbi. His story is really an inspiring one and I feel very proud of him and still feel that I share very deeply in his life. Sherril is a novelist and you can read about their life more in her various novels, which are wonderful to read. In 1992 or so Alan and Sherril moved to San Francisco where Alan is the rabbi at Beth Shalom, the Conservative synagogue on Fourteenth Avenue that I have driven past thousands of times on my way to meetings at the San Francisco Zen Center. For years I noticed the place and felt a warm feeling. Alan is a marvelous rabbi; his sermons are powerful and relevant and many people are discovering, through his inspired words and actions, the deeper possibilities of Judaism.

This morning, as I often do, I officiated at morning service here at Green Gulch. Carefully I go up to the altar where the large figure of Manjushri sits, and put the stick of incense in the big bowl full of ash. It easily goes in, just upright, not leaning to the right or left, in the exact center of the bowl. Everyone is sitting on cushions on the floor, chanting in low voices, while a drum is struck rhythmically. I have done this thousands of time and it is always the same. While I am chanting, my voice blending with everyone's voice, the smoke curling up from the incense, the face of Manjushri smiling, it feels as if there is no time, or as if time goes on endlessly.

THE DIASPORA MUSEUM

THE MORNING BEGAN SADLY: Hilda's front tooth fell out and it was really too bad — how could she go to Channah looking like this — she ran across the street to the dentist but no — then called — finally found the dentist worked in B'nei B'rak, that's where we have to stop on our way to Tel Aviv. It was a front tooth and Hilda had to hold her hand over her mouth the whole time, very embarrassing and uncomfortable.

But first an errand — to one local bank where my father is to deposit ten thousand dollars into Simon's account. It seems through various complex reasons having to do with black markets in currency and tax evasion, Eliezer, Simon's brother, was salting away USA dollars and needed to get a USA check from Simon so he could now deposit them; you can't deposit them in cash without paying heavy taxes. Anyway Simon sits on this cash for some time figuring to make money on the black market, but since inflation is now suddenly slowed to a halt in Israel, there is no more black market and he is stuck with this cash. The only way to deposit it is if it is done by a US citizen within eleven days of that citizen's arrival in Israel — so into the bank we all walk, my father carrying a small leather satchel, to deposit this money.

While we're waiting for the bank to check each bill for authenticity and to write down the serial number of each bill, Jeff and I watch the orthodox Jewish men wearing conventional bankers' clothing, tzizeth, (traditional fringed garments worn under the shirt) hanging out of their trousers around the waist, looking on the whole quite serious and purposeful as they do this and that, plying their ancient trade. We discuss politics.

It seems as if Danielle Weiss, head of the Gush Emunim, is being accused of stirring up a great deal of trouble around here lately. A band of settlers went into the Cave of Machpelah in Hebron (where Abraham is buried, now a mosque) and tore up Moslem prayer carpets. Their other vigilante activities, including an alleged petrol bombing in Qalqilya, are being perpetrated against a background of national news: Shimon Peres attempts to convene an international peace conference, against the strong protest of Shamir, the Prime Minister. How Peres, the Vice P.M., can carry on in public with such a plan unsupported by the P.M., I don't know: don't ask. This is after all Israel. That's the life. We note that curiously you have the same phenomenon happening here as in the USA — an alliance of the mass of middle class people who want ever bigger and newer homes in better developments with all the trimmings, with the political right, who will help them get it, and the religious fanatics who spice the whole pie with just enough hysteria to make it all a trifle frightening. In the USA you had, during the eighties, unprecedented wealth for the few, who may not have initially felt comfortable with right wing Reaganist views, but found themselves supporting those views for the personal advantage it brought them, aligned strangely with the Fundamentalist Protestant right; in Israel you have the more moderate settlers of Judea and Samaria, the West Bank, aligned with Likud and the fundamentalist Jews who believe that not an inch of "Jewish territory" can be given up to the Arabs. As Moishe said about Kahane (and Moishe is not a right winger), he's like Goldwater in the States, you don't support him but in your heart you know he's right.

At the Zen Center we are involved in a similar sort of debate: at what point does money, which is shorthand for a need for security, for normalcy, for the satisfaction of everyday wants, overturn the main purpose of what you are trying to do. Is money evil? The idealists might think yes, but really is the essential purpose of your religious practice or your righteous state going to be subverted if you have a little more? Probably not. On the other hand, if everyone has a big fancy house, three cars, VCR with cable and satellite, trips to Hawaii, and so on, will this change life's priorities? Probably, and this is something Israel will have to face as the idealism and almost desperate purpose that founded the nation gives way to the kind of lazy prosaic self interested slump that can come with mortgage, family, job security. Desperation, whether personal or national, is the great motivator. Without desperation, great vision and imagination is a lot harder to come by.

Banking done, off we go back to the house to pick up Hilda and things are very rushed nervous and hysterical as we must get out of the house post haste in order to make it to the dentist. We'll skip the physical therapist for my knees — oy, it's not easy getting old you can believe me — in order to make it to Tel Aviv we have to see everything! In order to make it to Hannah and Meyer's in order to...

B'nei B'rak — a very religious old town, mentioned in the Haggadah, the text recited at Passover seder, "when Rabbi Eliezer, Rabbi Joshua, Rabbi Elezer the son of Azariah, Rabbi Akiba and Rabbi Tarfon were sitting around all night discussing the departure from Egypt in B'nei B'rak," — which possesses the two main characteristics of all religious neighborhoods in Israel: lots of serious purposeful bearded men in black hats, lots of women wheeling baby carriages. The streets are crowded with both varieties as we window shop waiting for Hannah to get glued. We discuss the topic that most people will discuss in a foreign country: how much does it cost here, how much does it cost there, how much did you pay for it. In the windows when they display suits for the little boys they display kipot to match. The stores are all rather small and run-down but on the whole the town is pleasant. The streets are full of cars.

At Tel Aviv University we tour the Diaspora Museum, an institution dedicated to the proposition that Jews who do not live in Eretz Yisrael are human too. In fact a plaque or sign at the outset of the exhibition does say that the purpose of the museum is to see to it that there is a mutual understanding between Diaspora Jews and Jews living in the homeland since any misunderstanding or lack of mutual respect would be disastrous for both sides. Of course the need for such a museum only occurs when there is already a lack of mutual respect, when there is already the feeling that Jews in the Diaspora (a term of course that only exists at all with the assumption that all Jews really belong in Israel and are only temporarily displaced) are taking the easy way out. The Museum does not contain any bona fide artifacts or documents: it is all a fabrication, using the latest techniques of museum display and design, to show the history and culture of Jews, scattered in the four corners of the world. It is they say a five-hour situation, which we manage to complete in about three and a half hours of exhaustive museum stalking. An hour or two is my usual limit after which I feel ready to do something else but I manage to make it through. Many of the exhibits are not interesting but some cleverly use video or audio to good effect. In one, little fictional vignettes about Polish Jews and their relationship to Christian landed gentry and peasantry, which resulted in the long habit of anti-Semitism in that country, appear pantomimed by puppets, lit up in various areas of a large blackened proscenium, while you listen with earphones to a script that goes with the action; in another a conversation, hard through earphones, between a Jew and an Alexandrian in third century B.C. Museums are to educate the public, so if you know anything at all about the subject (and therefore are not "the public") it is quite simple-minded. But I can always learn more, and I do learn more, and besides, simple-minded is my favorite style.

There's a little film about Yeshiva life, as well as one about life in the shetl. This is very good: you sit down in a soft chair to watch in the dark. This, along with a computer that will give you the history of the town in Europe your family is from, or of the name you bear, occasions conversations about Ruskova, the original town of the Fischers.

Simon was a Yeshiva buchor there age thirteen-twenty, and life was exactly as the film describes, he says. Anyone living in Ruskova had to speak at least three languages — Romanian for school, Yiddish for at home and in the community, and Ukrainian for dealing with the local goyim. And if you were a Yeshiva buchor there you added a fourth — Hebrew of course. The boys all left their parents' homes to live together at the Yeshivot, but the Yeshivot did not feed them. Instead they were farmed out to various homes for eating and would make the rounds eating at one house on Tuesdays, one on Wednesdays, and so on. People in the community would "give days" to the bucharim as their fair share of support for this important religious practice, study, (in Gil's version of the millennium, the goyim work to support the Jews to study Torah — not that the Jews are in any way superior but just because you don't ask the foot to do the work of the head nor the head to walk, do you?) I ask Simon if he had intended to become a rabbi. No, he says. Then why study, I ask. To know, he says, very simply. His simplicity, evidenced in his sleepy half-open eyes, whose expression is always constantly mild and tolerant and open and innocent, is a most appealing quality in him, and it would be a remarkable, even an amazing quality, were it not so understated. One cannot imagine him arch, just as it is impossible to imagine him raising his voice. After the war, after the camps, his nearly forty years as a kosher butcher do not seem to have embittered him in the least; after all don't butchers have to keep the Jewish law to the letter, isn't that part of their job? The fact that Simon's real job has always been religion has made it possible for him I think to live cheerfully with an unsatisfactory situation. This is the wonderful thing, and the horrible thing, about religion, depending on how you look at it. I have always been impressed with the Jewish notion of the religious vocation, family, and an economic vocation existing side by side in one person, and in fact in Israel today there are many rabbis who earn their living in commercial trades, and this is in no way considered a disgrace. The early rabbinical saints themselves practiced in this way, most of them, as simple tradesmen. In any other tradition I know about, including Zen, the saints are on the whole single people, religious specialists, with no other social role.

The most moving exhibit in the museum for me, is something called the "In-gathering of the exiles." Stirring Israeli music plays while in a small odd-shaped vestibule down which the viewer walks, black and white slides of the settling of Israel are flashed onto the walls in a rhythm — you can see several parts of the slideshow simultaneously, First Aliya, Youth Movements, Kibbutzim. Tears strangely well up into my eyes — I say strangely but in fact this phenomenon of tears welling up when certain aspects of Judaism are recalled to me is not at all unusual, particularly since my mother's death. The feeling that I am "in exile," from what I can't say, and that I might return home, to where I can't say, to the state of Israel? to California? to Pennsylvania where I was born? to Ruskova where my grandfather was born? to death? — is something I think I feel, a feeling growing in me, which I think will perhaps occasion something sometime, I do not know what, or when.

I think of Judaism as a religion of life. In Judaism the dead are considered unclean and must be buried immediately — children are named for them to get them back into life as quickly as possible — there is not much sense of afterlife, rather the ongoing life of the community — and the Bible itself emphasizes hard work, prosperity, rain in season, if you behave in accord with the tradition, or, as our twentieth century American Jewish mamas have it, Be a Doctor, get Married, have Kids! And I think of Buddhism as a religion for death, with its meditations on death, especially the famous cemetery contemplations of the old tradition, the central importance of impermanence, emphasis on monkhood, doctrine of emptiness, renunciation.

But then again, Judaism, this great religion for life, has left a lot of people frozen, guilty, and afraid, unable to jump into life for fear of breaking God's rules; and Buddhism, this great religion for death, has become famous for fostering a broad free quirky enjoyable approach to life. Things are very confusing — maybe not things but just our way of thinking about them.

As Gil said at our Shabbat dinner in Jerusalem, A normal person doesn't need to meditate — only someone with a big problem needs to clarify that problem. And I always say to people, Please, if you already feel OK, if nothing is nagging at you or bothering you from the back, please, be happy as you are, don't let Zen practice disturb you.

But actually if you look at all deeply at life it is hard not to see big problems.

MYSTICS IN THE
GALILEE

THE NEXT MORNING WE ARE UP and piling into the car for our
trip to Tiberias. Despite the tremendous hospitality of Hilda and
Simon and the benefit of seeing a part of our family he never
knew existed, Dad is ready to go after these few days here. Everything is fine — as long as I follow all of Hilda's orders, he says.
She's strictly in control all the time, he says, and is glad we made
arrangements in advance for the Tiberias trip.

We drive with Simon to Kfar Saba to wait for the bus which
goes north through Hadera then northwest through Afula to
Tiberias. We pass some Arab towns along the way that look prosperous, but soon we are coming out of the cosmopolitan areas to
more modest terrain, small settlements, farms, into the Jezreel
plain with its wide fields, very fertile country on the other side of
the coastal mountains. Finally we approach the wide blue Sea of
Galilee (which is actually a lake), and the town of Tiberias in the
hills on its western shore. Once off the bus, tired and confused,
we are somewhat stymied by the fact that not much English is
spoken here and the place looks a bit seedy. Someone tells us our
hotel is five minutes away but it's actually pretty far away, up on a
hill overlooking the lake, which is good, but hard to get to town
from up here, which is bad.

I have a dislike for this hotel because you do not feel that it wants to be hospitable. People in the dining room don't feel like serving you, people at the desk don't like helping you with information, people in the tourist office in the town below, where we're walking around to check out the local scene, seem to feel that there are very few opportunities — come to think of it, there seem to be eerily no people in the hotel, nor on the streets are there many, and as we walk we pass many abandoned buildings, the town is not bubbling and cooking as Jerusalem is, it seems neither here nor there. We go to the tomb of Rambam, Moses Maimonides, which is hidden away (though it is supposed to be one of the town's main attractions) down some ill-used streets with empty industrial buildings — we have to go around the back way somehow, and once inside, we see a simple tomb on which a man is weeping. Other people are praying, and a lot of old guys who look pretty terrible are asking for charity. Back to bus station where we wait for a very long time for a bus to take us back to the hotel, we are quite tired and feel that special feeling that only a weary traveler in a foreign land knows: you don't speak the language nor know the place, everything seems disorganized and unsatisfactory, you are sure people don't care to speak to you and if they do they'll give you misinformation and if you try to buy something you'll be cheated, you feel in a word, very foreign, very alien — a way you feel generally your first day in a foreign city, when you are displaced and nervous about the arrangements, particularly a city like Tiberias that is not set up to accommodate the American dollar and the person who brings it.

Back to the hotel finally, we all take long naps, and we go to bed early too.

The next day we've arranged for a private tour of the Galilee with Amos Shapira, a dark young man with a new Volkswagen van he's quite concerned about. This van seems to stand for salvation, or the promise of the future, and a scratch on it could therefore diminish one's chances of escape to a better life. Amos is a very sympathetic person. You want to pay him extra for the tour not because he does it so well, though he is very nice, but because you're sure he needs it.

We're going to Zefat, city of the mystics. On the way we discover important things about Amos Shapira — from Tel Aviv, he moved here a few years ago because as an under-settled area the Galilee is subsidized by the government, and people are given quite liberal loans for settling here. His wife is a teacher; they have two young daughters. People say, he tells us, too bad, maybe try again for a son, but I say I wanted the daughters — look, I have to go forty days a year in the reserves, should I want also a child to have to do this...bad enough I have to give the forty days. And every year I go back to the same place — till age fifty-five! — and I am in the Air Force, which is the good service, better than the others. Although he is not supposed to talk politics, it is against the ethics of the tour guide, he makes others of his views clear to us: the politicians of today are nothing, they just want to make out, and today in Israel if you are elected to a second four-year term of the Knesset you are privileged for life, yes, Yigdal Allon was one of the great ideologues (we pass a museum for him in the kibbutz where he lived — in fact the Galilee area has many kibbutzim, founded early, it is a marvelous area for agricultural settlement what with the great natural beauty, the availability of water, the favorable climate — below sea level, so fairly warm year round — tropical fruit can be grown here). Begin was really a great man — even though I don't agree with him, still he is the last of the great politicians, though the ministers under him were not good. This area we are passing through now contains new private homes subsidized by the government for people who were evacuated from the Sinai when we gave it back to Egypt, here are older houses. I think the government made a big mistake encouraging the people to come here — because the government does not find them jobs and here there is not what to do (the fact that Amos is spending half his day on a tour for three people — we are not paying him terribly well — is testimony to this fact). There is so much tax even if there is what to do the tax is taking it all. The Jews in Judea and Samaria it is also a mistake because of the one million Arabs there. Let me tell you although I am not talking politics that my idea is a Jewish state, a small country with Jews in it. I am not interested to have the big problem of the million Arabs. I would first want to have peace if that is possible.

Along the road great beauty. Mountains above, fertile plain below, with mangrove, avocado, prickly pear, banana, wildflowers in bloom, beyond that the blue lake, very calm. From the peak of Mt. Hermon water flows from three springs into streams which join to form the Jordan which flows into the Sea of Galilee here, then out the sea and down the Jordan valley to the Dead Sea, finally out to the Red Sea. Here we are at Rosh Pinna, the first modern settlement in the Galilee, founded by Baron Rothschild. His managers did not get along with the settlers. Some settlers were killed during the riots of the 1920s.

We climb a great mountain to get to Zefat, quaint town of narrow terraced streets and great views. One of the four holy cities of Israel (with of course Jerusalem, and Hebron, and Tiberias). Nearby in the town of Meron is buried the famous Rabbi Shimon Bar Yohai, who escaped the Romans (second or third century) and spent thirteen years studying in a cave — he is said to have written the *Zohar* ("Brightness"), fountain of Jewish mysticism (though this book did not appear in the world until the twelfth century and was almost certainly written by Moses de Leon)— and thus the Jewish mystical rabbis of the sixteenth century, expelled from Spain, came here to the Galilee to found their Kabbalistic communities and still today you see their descendants, Chassids of various stripes, hurrying by in the streets, mixed up in and preoccupied with God. One can easily imagine the rabbis studying and arguing in these small hillside buildings — it seems the perfect place for it.

The Buddhist center that compares with this is Nalanda University, the great eighth century Indian monastic center, a huge complex of great temples and residences. Nalanda was the place where the forms and practices of Buddhism were fully developed, elaborated and refined. I imagine that place as lofty, rarefied, full of magnificent images, hieratic architecture.

Zefat isn't like this at all. It's a modest town, a village. Some houses stuck in the hillside; a street with stores and art galleries; some old synagogues. The synagogue of Joseph Caro is pretty small and unspectacular. Judaism is not noted as far as I know for sacred architecture and attempts at this in the modern period have been pretty sad. Jews don't seem to want a holy place: the temple was that, that's gone, and now we have, in effect, another religion, one which doesn't assume the divine as associated with any particular feeling or place. Joseph's synagogue is therefore a very small, human-scale, comfortable place, a place where men (and it is men) gather to study and debate, to pray and contemplate. No particular attempt is made to evoke the divine presence. You come in, you sit down, you pray, you get up, you go. And there is nothing religious or wonderful in this. It is just that, that is what you are supposed to do, and so it is what you do do. The marble pulpit is in the center of the small room, behind it a cabinet full of very old books. Ornate lamps are suspended from the ceiling over the pulpit. Deeply recessed windows look out onto views of the surrounding hillsides. Decorating the molding around the windows are simple designs, a star, a heart, a circle, in red, yellow-red, or white.

The synagogue of Isaac Luria is nearby. It's also very small (both these places would accommodate no more than thirty or forty worshippers, maybe twenty comfortably, though we're not going to be here for services) but within its small space there are nine small arches with white plaster pillars supporting them. The raised central pulpit is surrounded by railings painted yellow, green and brown. Its pillars are painted a streaky brown, with blue, yellow and green leaves at the tops of the columns. The ark is ornately painted also, but the painting is crude. The whole room has rather the effect of a home or a clubhouse than an exalted and holy spot. There are study tables all around in the open spaces surrounding the pulpits.

I feel comfortable doing religious practice in places like these, less comfortable in holy places that make me feel that something really important is happening. When I first began to practice Zen I went to the Zen Center in San Francisco where there were beautiful and expensive Buddha images, real treasures, purchased for the Zen Center by Zentatsu, who is, as I have said, a great purchaser not only of Buddhist art but also of art in general. He is very sensitive to the monumental, to the subtle power that architecture and art can have on the mind of the practitioner. Art is impressive; it dwarfs you; it makes you very receptive. His own house is full of art of all kinds crammed into every corner, and when he left the Zen Center one of the great but undignified aspects of it was a contentious consideration of the question of what belonged to him and could therefore be taken, and what belonged to the Zen Center. But I have never liked so much this power of religious art, or art of any kind, to influence us by the splendor of things. So I didn't even go to the San Francisco Zen Center to practice, instead I went to a small Zen center in Berkeley, which was located in the attic of an old Victorian house. The Buddha image on the altar there was about two inches high. It was easier to bow to than the bigger ones. Besides, the Buddha figure was bowing also to you as you bowed to him.

I think it is George Steiner who writes somewhere that when the Jewish culture was destroyed by Hitler in Eastern Europe it was gone without a trace. No ruins, no monuments, were left, because the Jews had put all of their creative energy into study and prayer and their way of daily life, and none of it into physical manifestations of their faith.

People think that Judaism is an ethical and rule-bound tradition without meditative elements, that the Kabbalistic teachings were wacky impossible to understand esoterica that stood in contradistinction to the dominant mode of the tradition. I don't think so. If you read the Bible and the prophets and the later mystical writers with the assumption that the God they are talking about is something they actually know about concretely and that you can know about this too if you make an effort to find out about it, then a lot of what you will read there begins to make sense.

Meditation is not a special state. It's an aspect of mind all the time that can be emphasized or heightened at certain times by chance, or intentionally. It involves a focusing or a clearing of the mind onto a single point and then finally no point at all. This kind of clearing out, or attention, is called "kavanah" in Hebrew, and has always been the main point of prayer in Judaism. Only we've gotten preoccupied with other things and have forgotten about it.

The trick about meditation is that it's not instrumental: if you are trying to get something out of it that intention prevents the deep clearing of the mind. Since meditation involves this giving over of intention to non-intention, to what is deeper than your intention or what is your real intention underneath your intention, it is always a religious act. It is not a technical thing.

The easiest way to work on this is with the body and the breath because they're so simple. But if you only work on it that way you leave out talk, and you can't get around talk, so you need teachings. Even in Zen which is supposed to be beyond talk there are teachings, some talk you need to get to, to get past, so you can clear things up.

But Judaism is all about talk in the beginning middle and end. So Jewish meditation has always been about language, and this is why Kaballah is so wacky, because it drops way down into language, into the essentially symbolic, to where language and the extra-linguistic are the same. But I don't think Kaballah is something unusual in Judaism; it's just an elaboration of the basic meditation on language, through language to God.

Rabbi Isaac Luria of Zefat wrote extensively on the Zohar, and showed how it was actually a way of meditation. A basic practice used by his disciples was to meditate on a Biblical verse, to hold it deeply in mind, breathing into it, writing out the letters slowly and carefully, immersing one's self in it night and day until one's intention and the verse became the same thing. Rabbi Joseph

Caro used the repetition of a verse from the Mishnah, on and on until, as he put it, an angel came and spoke to you. This is just the same as koan practice in Zen, where you internalize the koan until it speaks to you when you finally shut up.

I'm sure that the prophets, even the great earlier Biblical personages, were people just like us who spoke to God in this way. They may not have used these latter-day tools to clear the mind. Sometimes you don't need to. Sometimes things happen to you (a sudden face to face meeting with death; getting drunk; falling down and hitting your head on a rock) that bring it on. The Bible is a story about such things that happened. About people who, at a time when history demanded it of someone, were moved to ask deeply what is the point of being human. Things happened to them because of this.

This old tradition of Jewish meditation is just now coming back into vogue after a long time of being forgotten. It's pretty hard to get though because it is so embedded in the language and customs of elsewhere and the past. That's why so many Jewish people like Zen: you just sit there; you don't need to know Japanese.

The tradition was not forgotten by accident though. It was forgotten on purpose for two reasons I think: first, because it particularly separated the Jews from other peoples and a lot of Jews didn't like that because, among other things, it was dangerous; and second because some people got into trouble with these Jewish meditative teachings. There is the famous story of Sabbatai Tsvi who, in about the middle of the seventeenth century, rose up as the greatest teacher of Jewish mysticism, and therefore (this is logical in Judaism) as the Messiah. He marched in triumph on Constantinople to take over the world, was seized by the authorities and ordered to convert to Islam or die. He converted. Jews made a mighty attempt to expunge his name and all he represented from the tradition. A century later the Chasidic masters, revivers of the tradition, also fell prey to the cult of personality in many cases, so that the later Chassids tended to ignore or re-interpret the meditative elements of the tradition and emphasize other things.

That's the trouble with meditation: to go deeply into it you need a guide and you need to open yourself to the bottom. And then it is tricky whether you are in touch with something authentic or whether you have just in a marvelous, but in the end probably very dangerous, way covered the whole world with a thin veneer of your own big ego. So it's dangerous and people, gurus and teachers too, though well intentioned, get caught this way. There are many examples of this in our own time. My test is this: if you think you know something someone else doesn't, if you think you are different from someone else, be careful. If you think everyone you meet, even the nasty ones, even the ones who are caught, are buddhas, then you're probably OK. If being around your teacher makes you feel excited and exalted but deep down you feel badly about yourself there's probably something wrong. If your teacher makes you feel like you, just the mixed up way you are, are OK, then you probably have a chance.

That afternoon we tour (while Dad sleeps, one morning did him in) around the lake to the various Christian sites, as well as some kibbutzim. Amos very kindly shows us everything, but seems singularly to lack enthusiasm. He tells us his brother is in L.A. in the electronics business, doing well. He'd like to go too — at least just once to visit — his brother comes here once a year, every year — but his wife doesn't want to go. Here in Israel it is very hard because of the taxes. Then when you go into the army for forty days you don't get paid if you have your own business. It is very difficult to own your own in Israel. My brother warned me against this.

Many famous rabbis are buried in the area of Zefat and Tiberias. This is because they believe the Messiah will arise here first, not in Jerusalem. The whole Jerusalem phenomenon in fact comes up with David who conquered it and made it is his capital, 1000 B.C. — before that Jerusalem was not part of Israel and is of course not mentioned at all during the Mosaic period. David created the cult of the king — before David it was not at all clear that Israel was to be a kingdom with centralized rule — certainly, before and after the age of the kings, fighting and division among the people was the rule not the exception — and with it the cult of the Temple with Jerusalem as its holy seat. The early Zionists, in fact, despite the fact that a return to Jerusalem had for thousands of years symbolized the return to Zion itself, were not particularly interested in Jerusalem. It was too much trouble, fraught with too many political complications. Men like Herzl and Weitsman were neither religious nor sentimental: their idea was to found a modern nation state on the European model in land they felt they could make a strong legal claim to (they actively considered other places). Forget Jerusalem with its Christian and Moslem centuries. Tel Aviv, a blank slate ready to be what Zionism made it, was their idea of the heart and soul of the state of Israel. But since 1967 and the conquest of Jerusalem, and the rise of religious fundamentalism, this has changed.

Our little ride takes us to nearby Meron, where Rabbi Shimon is entombed. Every year on Lag B'Omer — and for a month beforehand — people come to gather here. As we drive up — Lag B'Omer is a few days away — the place takes on the air of a carnival or pilgrimage festival — tents everywhere, small booths, people selling pictures of holy rabbis, souvenirs, food, special prayer papers. Inside the tomb true believers are congregating, kissing the tomb of the Rabbi Shimon and his son Eliezer, praying no doubt for all good things to happen and no bad things. There are many legends connected with praying at this tomb. It is very much like the cult of the saint in Catholicism, and here there is the same excited fanaticism you find there, only here instead of a hushed holy feeling, you hear lots of talk, even arguing, in fact the place is pretty loud, more like a bazaar or a debating society or a living room in Brooklyn than the tomb of a saint.

Driving with Amos Shapira around the Sea of Galilee on a bright blue quiet day to the place where the great Jewish mystic Yashua (Jesus) taught.

The church at the site on the shore where Jesus predicted Peter would be the rock on which the future would stand — inside the small church, run by the Franciscans, a priest is giving a sermon; he looks very holy and gestures theatrically. In front of him is the very rock where Jesus stood. The church is right next to the water, a very peaceful spot.

The Church of the Multiplication of the Loaves and Fishes — a new church which incorporates the second century mosaic floor of the original church. A white mosaic with simple figures of birds, fish, it is the most beautiful mosaic floor I've seen in the Holy Land. Here too a rock on which Jesus stood is incorporated into the altar of the church.

We stop off at a kibbutz where Amos used to live for two years (as he drives us around he stops off at various kibbutz guest houses and hotels to deliver his fliers so he can drum up more business). He loved it. But his wife hated it. Now his wife would like to move back but he doesn't want to — not now that he has a five-room house.

We go back to the hotel where Dad, who's napped and awakened and is waiting for us, is very excited. He has a funny way of getting most excited just when Jeff and I are very tired. We go down to the hotel bar because there is really nothing else to do in Tiberias up on this hill far away from town. The bar is pretty unpleasant because they play bad music too loudly and the bartender is a strange burley man with a belligerent and crude personality — not wanting to get you anything (when there are few customers he sits in the TV room next door and you have to go get him if you want something), but then in the next minute insisting that you take two and getting pretty annoyed if you don't — and Dad goes on and on about his family, his father, the early days of the synagogue in Exeter, Pennsylvania, his girlfriend Lillian, as we drink beer and eat the queer cake that they give you while slouching down in the smooth almost edible-looking red and black plush chairs, in the room that can only be called a "lounge."

Though I have a good one now, I have not always had a good relationship with my father. Sometimes when I was growing up we fought or didn't even bother to fight so soured were we on each other. Actually we didn't know each other very well, and in the absence of our knowing one another we were left only with the deep images in our minds, "father," and "son," and we didn't realize it. "Father" is loving yourself, finally approving of yourself. "Son" is securing your place in the world, being worthy of admiration. None of it worked out very well. And it was even worse with my mother and she is dead now. So I am very happy to be drinking beer here with my father, in one of his rare moments of enthusiasm and an almost beside himself excitation of conversation in which the whole world brightens up and no matter what he's talking about even if he's complaining about his friends, who take too many pills and worry about themselves too much or worry about him too much and won't leave him alone, or about his relatives, who don't fulfill their family obligations as they ought to and meddle in each other's affairs and have funny ideas about money — it is, like a litany or a song, itself a redemption, just the talk, just the being listened to, just the sound of the words in the air between us, father and son.

At moments like these my father is a very handsome man. He's not a wise man but he is a simple and straightforward one, no aspirations, no pretensions, just delighted at seeing what can be seen and accepting what can be had in this life.

He tells me about his nap-time dream: Sam Sumner was somehow cheating him at business. He got mad at Sam but couldn't find him to complain and so in his frustration he kicked out a window. On the other side of the window there was a dance-floor, and then he was dancing, gliding over the floor, with Mom. She was such a beautiful woman, especially when she was young, when they first met at Sandy Beach, and it was one look, just one, and bam, that was it for life, and she always did look exactly that way to me ever since, even when she got older she looked the same way underneath how she looked, if you know what I mean. Now that I am talking about dreams it reminds me that I always have this dream about working for Prudential. I am on my collection route and all of a sudden I am stopped on the road by a big boulder in the road. One falls behind me one is in front of me. I can't go forward and I can't go back. I am stuck there on the road and time is going by and I have got to get my collections done. Time is coming in from the sides and from above, pressing down on me, and I'm not moving, not getting anywhere. It builds up and it builds up. Pretty soon I can feel it pressing down on me right here, in my chest. Usually that's when I wake up. I never told anyone about that. Boy that's some dream.

I am thinking of my father as one of the mystics of the Galilee: a spiritual hero just to have survived these sixty-five horrible years of human history, to have lived to tell about it.

WHICH ONE IS THE JEWISH ONE

WE'RE TIRED OF THE HOTEL, its bleakness and eerie quietness. The first day there was a Christian group, very cheerful, all wearing T-shirts that said "I was baptized in the River Jordan." They were pretty enthusiastic. But since then the dining room has been very quiet and the food is no good so we've come down the hill outdoors and into the weather to see what we can find. There's a little restaurant down the street but no one's in there either. Is it closed? We stand outside looking in, and, as usually happens around here when you look with interest into a shop from the street, a man comes out to encourage us to come in, the food is very very good, he says, and it is cheap. The place does serve St. Peter's fish, the local fare, which we want to eat, so we go in, sit down at a booth. Jeff and I order the fish. Dad orders chicken. This is what he always orders. It is what he lives on, chicken and corn flakes, and occasionally noodles. He has never been a particularly adventuresome person, in the mouth or anywhere else. And it is worse now that he has chronic incurable hepatitis that he got from a bad blood transfusion after his last heart by-pass. So it is chicken, which he munches reflectively. The fish is deep fried.

We discuss at length and frankly the question of the Jewish upbringing of our children. Dad wants me to have bar mitzvahs for Aron and Noah when they are thirteen — he feels these may be the only bar mitzvahs he'll attend of his grandchildren (Simon, Jeff's son is six, Hannah is nine). I explain that this is a big problem because in fact (according to all but the reform Jews) the children are not Jewish because their mother is not Jewish and would need to convert and this is in itself a complicated arrangement that would, in fairness, involve the children being old enough to really choose to do it. And I'm not sure they would choose to do it, nor am I sure how Kathie would feel about it if they did. It's a delicate matter, I explain. And this is not even considering the practical difficulty of my being a Zen priest living in a Zen Center. I hardly make any money and how would I pay for Hebrew lessons or find the time to drive the children the distance from the center, which is well out of town, to some synagogue or school. The meditation schedule is really demanding. Besides, even if I were able to do all of this how could we ever afford to hold the bar mitzvah in a synagogue where they charge a lot of money and anyway don't know us and if they did would become confused by it all, and if we had the bar mitzvah at the Zen Center this would even be more confusing and even upsetting to the students there.

When we studied a few years ago in the New York Zen community with Tetsugen-sensei (aka Bernie Glassman from Brooklyn) we did have the experience of mixing up religions. There an important side of the practice was ecumenicalism, and there were special Jewish Zen retreats during the High Holy Days. They actually had Jewish services in the Zen Center, had their own Zen rabbi, an old friend and student of Bernie's. Every Shabbat there was a big dinner and all the Zen students had to put on kippot and celebrate. I remember one of the monks there, Kosho, a Japanese guy, sitting at the table every Friday night wearing a kipah. He usually looked very confused and glum on those occasions.

Jeff on the other hand does have Jewish children who clearly identify as such. Hannah in particular is concerned to the point of obsession with being a Jew. But Jeff is not at all sure that he and Ellen are willing to do what it would take to provide the children with a Jewish upbringing. Their way of life — in Maine with many non-Jewish friends, living a life centered on the out-of-doors, on exercise and health — does not mesh easily with typical Jewish life in America, and joining the local synagogue (which they are debating doing) they fear would involve time commitments and social commitments which they are unwilling to make. Besides, Jeff doubts the usefulness of all this Jewish education. Would his own youthful time have been better spent studying piano than going to Hebrew school, or synagogue, as he did do? Would a present ability to play piano be more valuable to him today than what vestige he has now of that Jewish education? Actually, he has a great regret about not knowing how to play the piano well, and it is too late now. Did he give that up for a God that stood by while millions of people were murdered and who even now seems to provide more, not less, violence. And besides — they give you rote learning, no sense of meaning or depth. And perhaps in the end one's Judaism is better served by less rather than more education, the education perhaps leads you in the direction opposite Judaism — you rebel against it. So bar mitzvah, rather than the beginning of participation in Jewish life as it is designed to be, becomes in fact the end of it — graduation, exemption from any real religious obligation.

But I feel as if my children could go to Hebrew school; if there weren't all these complications, I would surely send them.

Dad seems to have little to add to this discussion. His point seems to be he'd like to attend some bar mitzvah before it's too late to attend any.

He seems to have no use for what he calls "born again" Jews, religious Jews. He thinks adherence to Halakah (Jewish law) is a little nuts. Judaism seems to him to be a little like our team, our family, versus your team, your family. He's not that interested in it otherwise.

One of the great debates in Israel lately, the one that has finally roused American Jewry enough to open lobbying offices in Israel, is the one about who is a Jew. The fundamentalists in Israel, who hold the balance of power in the Knesset, want to exclude Reform Jews and any converts who have not been converted according to the tenets of orthodoxy. They want to keep Judaism pure, according to their idea of what is pure, but the American Jews have given a lot of money and sweat to Israel and they do not want to give up a piece of their Jewish identity. They do not want to feel like they are kicked off the team or in danger of soon being cut from the team. Anyway, it is their team in the first place.

It is very confusing who is a Jew. Someone might think like a Jew and practice like a Jew and not be one but someone else might do nothing a Jew does and dislike being a Jew and not consider himself a Jew but in fact be a Jew. But maybe not. I would say that this is just a confusion about names, and it is that, but I do not want to trivialize it because many people feel that the meaning of their lives is at stake with the turning and twisting of names. Names identify us.

I would explain Judaism perhaps as a very elaborate way of life, based on mindfulness, awareness of the absolute in all occasions, and the creation of a community very rigorously based on this awareness. There is a strength in this kind of life that gives nothingness (God) higher consideration than what is practical or desirable from one's own point of view. It makes perfect sense to me since one's own viewpoint or convenience is always shifting — only nothing remains fixed.

I remember some years ago answering a question put to me by my mother, who was dying at the time. She asked me what do Buddhists teach about dying? (We were eating bagel and cream cheese at the time in a fast food breakfast place outside Miami — it was a moment we carved out to spend together, and here we spent it among the formica tables, the grumbling customers, in the sweltering heat of a southern Florida summer.) I said that in

Buddhism we are finding out who we actually are, our face before our parents were born, and this face, this person, doesn't die and is never born. So although we don't want to leave this beautiful world we know that really we can't leave anyway — and that we were never here in any substantial or fixed way in the first place. While this seems to be really a trick of logic (since we know we are here, and we know people leave — we have experienced their loss) it is in fact a concrete reality, an actual experience. We really can have a sense of a deeper identity, one that remains clear and firm underneath, alongside of, or shot through our more usual, ephemeral identity. But my mother did not seem able to grasp nor to find consolation in this idea — in any case she was not asking for consolation since she posed the question as an academic one; she did not admit that she was dying, and she never did admit it — and she received my explanation with the awkward gesture she often made — and made even during her dying — of her upturned palm slicing the air at an oblique angle, a gesture that expressed something between "so what" and "goddamn it" and "Oh, I don't know, I just don't know."

Another time, again during the period in which my mother was dying, I questioned Rabbi Maza, my old friend and teacher, about this. What do you tell people when they are about to die, how do you console them? (We were in a restaurant in Manhattan having coffee and Danish, we were sitting intimately at a booth near the back, the Rabbi, dressed in a dark suit, was wearing the neat black hat he usually wore indoors and out.) His answer was that he reminds them that their children will carry on, the community will carry on, that they will live in the others who will carry their names or their work forward.

This is also a good explanation and will I think be more generally consoling to people.

The fish was deep fried, a bit greasy, yet without that much taste, but pleasant enough to eat. Dad said the chicken was fine, but he doesn't notice food much anymore. The point is, I said to Jeff (Dad wasn't listening), Judaism is a revealed religion. It is the word of God, absolutely, as transmitted to the Jewish people, who are chosen to receive it, and what they do with it, the struggles and trials they must undergo in the midst of it give them a tremendous sense of destiny.

Buddha on the other hand is more like a scientist or physician. He discovered a good way for people to be happy, found a language to describe the root of our human disease and a way to cure that disease. Buddhism in this sense is not "truth." More like "medicine." Any description of reality would probably do, so long as it is administered properly, with a clear enough understanding of the underlying logic of salvation....this is why Buddhism is so tolerant, so open-minded.

Jeff allowed as how this attitude seemed so much preferable to him than the more hysterical notions of the Jews. But I myself also have a taste for the vengeful, ambitious, difficult God who creates such disturbing and dramatic historical difficulties.

Next day I phoned Tamir from the hotel while Dad and Jeff ate breakfast. Our procedure has been to pack everything very carefully the night before so we can be off quickly the next day. Dad is very anxious about packing, packing efficiently, traveling light, being on time, being early, doing it all right, and it is when we are about to move that he gets into these things in a serious way, he becomes a little nervous, a little hard to take, but only a little. Jeff and I kid him and tease him — we both think he's nuts! — but of course also recognize ourselves in him, and very much so. Were he not behaving this way probably we would have to. And at other times, when he gets excited and talkative, or when, as at the conclusion of our trip, he explained to his sister all about it, he smiles and seems very breathless and boyish, very charming and appealing. One's father is never an ordinary person. This seems to be the logic of human generation. One's father, as you see him from across a room, at a distance, with others, or nearby, alone, has always got to be an enigma of one's self, a difficulty.

Tamir is a young kibbutznik who is wondering what to do

with his life and in the course of his travels came to Green Gulch. But he couldn't quite do the practice. Yearned to do it, or to do something, but because of his background could not.

It had been one of my plans in Israel to visit Tamir at his kibbutz, to try to talk to people there, if possible, about Zen. But as it developed, in Israel I forgot all about Zen (the Jewishness here so thick, so deep and pervasive, there does not seem room or reason for anything else), as though it never existed. When people asked me what I did, particularly my orthodox relatives, I only told them that I managed a collective farm (which was true) and left out the Zen part, not wanting to deal with the necessary explanations, embarrassment, or alienation. And, as it turned out, Tamir was in any case not living at the kibbutz — he was in Tel Aviv, working in the film industry. I'm trying to find out if I fit in here, he said over the phone. It's good to hear your voice, he said. People here need some Zen talk. But it was too complicated to arrange a meeting — particularly since everything I did had to be worked around Dad, who has a low tolerance for what is out of the ordinary, represents a schedule change, or is inconvenient, not to mention costly, and so I gave up on the idea. Perhaps there will be another trip to Israel — surely there will be another trip — time, a life may quickly go by, but somewhere in some time zone, for someone in one way or another there is always another trip to Israel.

ON SUNDAY

Every Sunday at the Green Gulch Zen Center there is a public period of meditation in the morning followed by a public talk. Because we are very close to San Francisco and have been here a long time and done a great many things many people know about us and they come on Sunday to meditate and to hear the talk. Our parking lot is a large open flat space under hills next to a small pond. Every Sunday it is filled with cars. The lecture hall is an old barn which is also filled every Sunday with people who have heard many Zen talks before, and also with many newcomers. I think we must be in some tourbooks so new people are always coming.

One Sunday it was my turn to give the talk. I always talk about the same thing: about how our human life is very deep and wide, we're not actually in control of it or able to understand it fully, but our minds are full of narrow conceptions about who we are and what life is, and the difference between our narrow conceptions about the way things are and the way they actually are creates suffering in ourselves and everywhere else. So we have to meditate, not just as a way to calm ourselves down or relieve our stress, but as a way of breaking through our narrow conceptions into a wider and more imaginative life. I often talk about the imagination. People are sometimes surprised because they think that Zen is about being in the present moment and that being in the imagination is the opposite of being in the present moment.

After the talk we serve tea on the deck outside the lecture hall and after a while we go into a smaller room, surrounded with windows, where the speaker for the day answers questions and engages in dialog with the listeners.

On this Sunday Ruth Kaufman, a cheerful white-haired woman in her seventies who comes nearly every Sunday, asked me about a Catholic convent located next to the ruins of the Auschwitz death camp in Poland that had recently been in the news. She explained the situation to me. She said that the convent had had a cross erected, a cross clearly visible from the camp, almost as though it were part of the camp, and that Jews both locally and internationally were outraged at the insensitivity of this. The local Bishop had intervened and a compromise had been worked out whereby the convent would remain but would remove the cross and set itself up instead as an ecumenical retreat center. But then the Bishop had gone back on this compromise and reaffirmed the place as a Catholic convent. The Catholic nuns were there expressly to pray for the souls of the Jews who had been killed at Auschwitz. They could not understand why the Jews had a problem with this. Were the Jews being narrow minded? Were the Catholics being stubborn? Ruth wanted to ask me, she said, because she wanted to get the opinion of someone who was neither Christian nor Jewish.

I was sitting up on the couch in meditation posture, wearing my robes, with my head shaved, as it usually is. What makes you think I am not a Christian and a Jew? I said to her.

Well, Ruth said, I mean I just wanted to ask someone who isn't emotionally involved.

Why do you think I'm not emotionally involved? I asked her.

Then someone asked about the Japanese forms in our meditation hall. How come there is all this bowing and all these robes and incense? Does it make sense to have these Japanese things when none of us are Japanese?

I put my palms together to show her the traditional gesture the Japanese call "gassho." Is this Japanese or not? I said. Actually when I do it I don't know what it is. I have been doing this gesture and wearing these robes for almost twenty years, practically my entire adult life, I said. It doesn't seem Japanese or unusual to me. Besides, the Japanese got it from the Chinese. And the Chinese got it from the Indians, and I don't know where the Indians got it from. When I put these robes on and do gassho it just feels pretty ordinary. I am just a regular Jewish guy from a little town in Pennsylvania doing what I have done almost my whole adult life.

Then someone else asked about how to deal with anger especially when someone really is out to harm you. Turning the other cheek seems stupid, he said. And getting angry and fighting back doesn't seem to work out either. What is the Buddhist way to do it?

It's really amazing how many people have trouble with anger.

Well, I said to him, you really have to take yourself in hand and be a good teacher for yourself. First of all you have to really be convinced that being angry is not a good thing for you or anyone. Maybe you have to get angry enough to see that, to see all the harm it causes. Or maybe you can just reflect on it, think about it over and over again or read good texts about it until you are really convinced that anger doesn't help. Then when you get angry instead of complaining to yourself about what a bad person you are to get angry or justifying yourself to yourself about how the person really deserves your anger because they are so rotten or maybe how your anger will help straighten them out and your hatred will be good for them, you have to just look and say, yes, this is anger. Anger is no good and I have made a commitment to stop following the way of anger, but this is definitely anger. There it is. This is how it feels. This is how it arises. This is what happens. And then you don't do anything. You don't act in anger. You don't try to make the anger go away or pretend it's not anger. You just notice it. And if you train yourself like this, over and over again, pretty soon, like a fire that has no more fuel, your anger will die down and finally burn out. Sometimes you'll get angry. But probably less often.

People think that our thoughts or our mind is us. But actually our thoughts are just our thoughts and our mind is just our mind. So we have to take care of our thoughts as we would a child because our thoughts get mixed up and troublesome sometimes. The *Dhammapada* begins, "What we are today comes from our thoughts of yesterday and our present thoughts build our life of tomorrow: our life is the creation of our mind." So we have to be careful of our thoughts.

(I say things like this over and over again because I have tried them out and I know they work and in the hope that someone will believe it and put it into practice.)

Then there was, as there often is and often has been in the more than fifty years since Zen has been seriously practiced in the West, a long discussion about the similarities and differences between Zen and psychology. Psychology is about the self, I said. About how to take care of it, how to free it from sticking points, so that it can be successful. Zen is about the self too, but it looks at the self from the standpoint of the darkness that surrounds the self or is in the middle of the self. Our usual method is to plunge you right into this darkness and forget about the details. But this isn't always so good. Maybe, having ignored the details about the self, we've created a way that favors deep but neurotic practitioners. Maybe we've created a way that doesn't help as many people as well as it could, or should. But psychology has its limitations too because if you just work with the self and ignore the darkness then you can't really help the self to heal. There is some healing. But if you are still stuck with the self just as self there will always be a deep and unresolved problem. Actually, if you want to really heal the self you have to throw it away. So maybe Zen and psychology aren't really two different things but just aspects of one thing. Maybe there are really no such things as "Zen" or "psychology." Just living. Or maybe saying "living" is already making a mistake.

Then someone said, I liked what you said this morning about the imagination and about how we need to decide to take a leap in our lives, out of our ordinary habitual way of living and into a deeper life of the imagination. But how do you do this?

Just then the lunch gong sounded really loudly and a woman who had fallen asleep in her chair during the discussion jumped up startled and everyone had a good laugh about that and there was a wonderful easygoing feeling in the room. It was a beautiful day outside; the slanting late fall light was coming in on us gloriously through the large windows that surround the room.

There is no way to do it, I said.

THE GOLAN

THE GOLAN HEIGHTS REGION, captured during the '67 war, and later annexed to the state of Israel, is one of the most beautiful and fertile regions of the Middle East. North of the Galilee, overlooking it and rising to a height of over ten thousand feet at Mt. Hermon, it is full of hills and valleys. Before the war the Israeli settlements in the Galilee, just at the border with Syria, were easy prey for artillery placements in the Golan. The Syrians apparently would sit up in the Heights and shell the settlements daily. So the capture of the Heights was of paramount importance to the Israelis — and they accomplished this in two days that summer — the two day war, as Yehuda, our tour guide, calls it.

As we drive around the Sea of Galilee Yehuda describes the landscape and its history. A wiry man of about sixty or sixty-five, he enjoys giving explanations.

Ladies and gentlemen. Look please now at the route that Jesus took from Nazareth to Capernaum. I have not made this trip but my friend has told me that he has walked this trip in six hours. So please ladies and gentlemen do not imagine that this walk has been such a very difficult walk.

Ladies and gentlemen please listen to me. The waters of the Sea of Galilee irrigate the Negev. There is a pipeline that is to do this but it depends upon good rainfall to fill the streams that feed the Jordan River. Look please at the pumping station which here is built underground for the security reason. For the last three years there has been a drought in Israel. When I say drought I mean that the Sea was very very low — ladies and gentlemen I have lived in Tiberias all of my life and I want to tell you that I have not seen the waters so low. I would say we are having a very serious problem and it would be necessary for us to do something — we might have to import water. This is not a joke. But — thanks God this year the rains were very great and now as you can see for yourself there is fullness in the lake and as you can see the Jordan River is very full and even now still a lot of water is coming down from the mountains and flowing into the Jordan River. Even from the very beginning of Jewish history there is great difficulty because of the water and because of the water also there is fighting. The problem is not that people hate one another but it is very important for who will eat what who has control of the streams and of the springs. Even today in the prayers of the Siddur you will hear of the asking for rain. And when there is not enough rain there may be more fighting than there was before...

The amount and variety of crops that grow here in the Galilee region is tremendous. We pass, in addition to a tremendous plethora of wildflowers — yellow of yarrow, purple of digitalis, white of wild carrot, pink of thistle, purple lupine, blue larkspur — mango groves, banana groves, avocado groves, olive groves, grapefruit groves, vineyards, and as we move higher, wheat, and elsewhere in the country cotton, squash, melons of all kinds, figs, dates, apples, oranges — I cannot think of anything that does not grow here. The fields are beautifully laid out, nestled in little valleys among the green (this time of year) hills. Beside many of the groves of fruit trees we see high piles of boulders that have been taken from the fields. We pass many kibbutzim — sometimes one right next to another, along the road, neat buildings clustered together with fields all around. These were founded in the 1930s, when the urgency that resulted in the final (if it is final) success of Zionism began to gather steam, with the hostility of the Arabs growing more boisterous, and the rise of Nazism more and more deadly. And it is these kibbutzim, close to the border, that bore the brunt of Arab hostility in the early years of the founding of the state.

We cross the Jordan over a Bailey bridge. Ladies and gentlemen listen to me now, Yehuda says. Look please at the Jordan River which we are crossing — this before the '67 war was the border with Syria. Ladies and gentlemen, the Syrians fortify themselves as the Russians do — they make five fortifications one behind the other. In case you get past the first there are still one and one and one and one to go. Here you see the first fortification. It seems the Syrians were careful to tell us where the fortifications were. When I say the Syrians were careful to tell us where their fortifications were, I mean they planted eucalyptus trees around each bunker. These trees grow quickly tall and are very unusual here. And so it was really quite easy to find the fortifications. If you like you can walk through one bunker and you can see, looking down from here onto the fields below, how easy it was for the Syrians to control the kibbutzim with their artillery.

We view the large concrete monument, in the shape of an airplane tail wing, and below it the stone slab on which are written the names of the fallen soldiers. The word "fallen" is always used to speak of soldiers who have been killed in battle. "Dead" is not used. "Fallen" sounds like the opposite of raised, what you'd do with a flag. And there is a monumental sadness in this word "fallen." It is heroic. Like a great tree falling, a huge weight, but without any sound. There are small stones placed on the marker, the way, at a funeral ceremony, Yehuda explains, we put a handful of dirt on the casket. All around the monument are cast-iron anti-tank obstacles, painted black. A little beyond it, overlooking the beautiful valley below, is a stone with a Hebrew inscription that reads "You are the bravest of the brave." This refers to the settlers below, who for so many years lived under the shadow of the guns that were here. This peaceful hillside, which reminds me so much

of the California hillsides I know so well — it is difficult to
believe that fighting has occurred here ever since Biblical times —
apparently King David waged campaigns in these hills against the
Edomites, or some other people of the area. And as we go on
past the other four Syrian fortifications we can see more war
memorials, usually incorporating a tank or an artillery piece,
always with the names of the fallen included. Israel is full of these
monuments, which do not suggest so much the glory of battle as
the determination to survive — these fell that we may stand. (I
do not intend to use patriotic rhetoric in speaking of the State of
Israel, but I have seen these monuments everywhere — piles of
stones stacked one on the other, a line of gravestones enclosed by
a granite arch, a machine gun with angel wings — and if I try to
write about them this is what comes out, and I see these young
people on the busses and in the towns carrying guns, and think of
my own relatives murdered in the Holocaust, and of course I can
also think, why do we bother to keep this up, and, it is only our
own stubbornness that causes this, and, if we were actually concerned with peace and not with territory and our own security so
hysterically so unfairly it wouldn't be so. This is the result of a
stubborn refusal to be like other people — to listen to other
people — to be concerned about other people — our insistence
in fact to be better than other people — all this I know, yet when
I write about it it comes out this way).

Ladies and gentlemen, Yehuda goes on, do not be surprised
when I say the Syrians who defended these positions were
chained to their guns — this is how the Syrian command got
them to stay and not to flee. If they were not chained to their
guns they were gone quickly from these positions.

I wonder if the Syrian soldiers actually cared one way or
another about the Jews in this place. Did they fire the guns
because they wanted to kill people or because someone told them
to? Did they run away because they were afraid or because they
didn't care to stay? Did they really run away or did they only run
away in Yehuda's version?

155

In 1981 the Golan was annexed to the State of Israel and now this twelve hundred square kilometer area has more than thirty new settlements that contain about nine thousand people. But unlike Judea and Samaria, the West Bank, which has a huge Arab population, the Golan was not heavily populated by Syria. Now, in 1994, Israel and Syria are engaged in the fitful stop and go process of peace negotiations, in which the return of some portion of the Golan is at issue. It is amazing that the Israelis are willing to seriously consider ceding some of this area; it will be very dangerous for them.

We pass one town, Quneitra, which is deserted. Before the war it had a population of twenty thousand people. In the disengagement agreement with Syria of 1974 Israel gave it back to Syria, but Syria did not repopulate it because it wanted also the four hills around it which control it. But Israel would not give the hills. So Quneitra is an abandoned town on the Syrian border, and we stand among the brilliant wildflowers on a hill overlooking the town and can see the Israeli fields that come right up to the city limit. One of these fields is a bright red carpet of anemones.

I bend to look at the brilliant purple lupines that grow by the side of the road.

As I write the pink clouds pale over the stone buildings and masses of TV antennae of the Old City of Jerusalem.

Maybe I won't ever write another sentence about Israel. Maybe that was my last sentence ever about it. But somehow I feel I am stuck writing about Israel, although here in Japan, sitting in the monk's quarters of Rinso-in temple, in Yaizu, with the sliding door open overlooking the carp pond that Suzuki-roshi made many years ago, Israel seems very far away, and beside the point.

There is something about writing itself. I have known people who knew a lot, then I have read books they wrote about what they knew and the books were much less than who they were and what they knew. But there is something about writing a thing down — it does not really tell you anything about what happened before the time of the writing, it is independent of that, but it has a power to it, because it includes the silence of what happened before, and what will happen later, the silence that surrounds the human need to speak, to explain. Human civilization begins with writing. Ladies and gentlemen please listen to me.

Our tour takes a break at the town of Qasrin which appears suddenly as a mass of pre-fab apartment houses and a shopping center in the middle of the mountain country. The government has encouraged settlement here by (1) exempting people from taxes for several years (a not considerable advantage, since as I have said Israeli taxes are sky-high), (2) offering them low interest long-term loans for cheap housing (also not inconsiderable since as I have said housing is very scarce and dear) and (3) offering long term interest-free loans for starting up businesses or industry in the area. The government is obviously very interested in getting loyal citizens into this annexed territory. Israelis are somewhat restless people always on the lookout for a new frontier (one suspects, as several people have told me, that the country is far too small to contain the economic and territorial ambitions of the Israelis) and so it has not been difficult to find settlers for Qasrin. Here we stop for a drink, go into a gallery, and buy some small primitive-looking statues, to give as gifts, made by Jews of the Ethiopian community who have recently immigrated to Israel. Afterward we tour the rather modest local museum of artifacts from the Golan. It seems that once the Israelis take on new territory they immediately dig it up for evidence of their past inhabitation there. Is it curiosity that makes them do this? Thirst for knowledge? Is it the excitement of possessing something long desired and only lately acquired? Is it an attempt to justify territorial conquest? Or is it another form of restlessness, another example of the wandering, in this case through time, that has been characteristic of the Jewish story since the exile from the Garden of Eden. In any case, the museum shows us photographs and models of Gamla, a place described by Josephus during the

Roman Period as on a hill overlooking a fertile valley, a synagogue and fortification that was strategic in those days. As always, the discovery of the place was a great detective story involving first the certainty (via Josephus, who is an extremely reliable source) that the place was there to be found, followed by the fruitless search, and then one day quite unexpectedly... Josephus himself, as Jewish commander of the Galilee forces in the revolt against Rome in the first century A.D., defended Gamla. When he was defeated, as the story goes, rather than be put to death he went to Rome, became a Christian, and worked for the government, eventually taking on the name of Josephus Flavius, after the General to whom he surrendered. The Bezak guidebook (an Israeli publication) refers to him quite directly as a "turncoat" but Yehuda points out that in fact were it not for Josephus we would not have so much history of the Jewish people of that period as we do, so much unbiased and accurate history. Perhaps he was a turncoat or a coward concerned only for his own hide, or perhaps he believed it was foolish to die resisting the inevitable tide of history, or perhaps he had a great deal of perspective and understood that unless someone survived, someone in a position to write about what had happened, the story would be lost to the Jewish people forever. It is difficult for me to see him as a traitor, rather I see him as a survivor, a clear voice speaking, and refusing to stop speaking, describing, participating.

Now I am just back from Israel, in Manhattan, the Upper West Side, in the apartment of my old friend, Rabbi Alan Lew, and I am writing this and looking out the window at the drizzly day and enjoying the excessive heat that comes blasting out of the pipes and reading here and there in Alan's books. One of them, Robert Alter's *Defenses of the Imagination: Jewish Writers and the Modern Historical Crisis*, says, "Language is the one artistic medium that develops perceptibly through historical time, bearing the marks of past uses upon it, and thus literature is before all others the memory-laden art, the one that resumes its past in the very act of exploiting its felt resources for the expression of the present...The possession of a past, then, is a necessary condition for the imagination of the future, the vaster and more varied the past, the richer the possibilities of the future will be..."

Josephus, back there then, must already have known about this, must have thought about it on his way to Rome, just as I think about it too, in my own confusions about time and place here at my desk in California some years after my trip to Israel. And in this knowing, both of us, Josephus and I, find ourselves at once at the same place, in the same time.

And when you read this you are there too.

SHABBAT DINNER WITH CHAIM

O UR EVENT FOR THIS DAY is Shabbat dinner with Chaim Ngori, brother to Schlomo, my cousin Karen's boyfriend.

Chaim lives in the orthodox section of Jerusalem, near Me'a Shearim, and works as a scribe.

Dad is complaining and avoiding if possible this engagement — who knows what crazy things Yemenite Jews are going to be into? They are practically Arabs, he imagines — or at the very least they are born-again Jews. Who knows what they'll serve for dinner or what stuff he'll expect us to do. He complains a lot and hopes Jeff and I will offer him a good excuse, but we don't.

We get off the bus at Me'a Shearim and wander through the market street looking for Joseph Caro Street, but no one seems to have heard of it — although it is only about two blocks away — we go in around the back to the house where a young pregnant woman who speaks no English (none of the people in this neighborhood seem to) invites us in, gives us some beer, and continues mopping the floor in the next room. We sit quietly in a large room with a high ceiling, very plain, with old world furniture, waiting for Chaim, who is phoned, Jeff speaks to him, he'll be here in a minute. Dad notices the small television set under the hanging plant and says, Oh, television — so it couldn't be so bad.

Chaim appears — small dark plump man in dress slacks and white shirt — fairly bursts onto the scene. Sorry to be late, come sit down, come in here, have to drink, oh you had to drink, please to sit, watch television (he turns on the television to an Israeli game show), introduces us to his mother, a very beautiful dark woman of not more than fifty who also speaks no English, then disappears. For the next hour or so he comes in and out to switch channels (at one point we are watching the videotape of his wedding, a traditional Yemenite wedding — it appears the young woman who had greeted us at the outset is his wife; at another point we are watching The Love Boat, which Dad rather enjoys — it's the first real TV in almost two weeks). Jeff is beginning to wonder whether it was in the end such a good idea to come here. Dad is falling asleep.

Chaim bursts back into the room and off we go — Jeff and I and Chaim — Dad lies down for a nap with elaborate arrangements, pillows, blankets, etc. by mother and wife — for a walk around the neighborhood.

Chaim's English is not so good — he's out of practice. He sometimes thinks of words but cannot remember so he has to explain the word, then we all try to guess which word he means — then when we get it he says, "exactly," while pointing his finger at us as though we were playing a game of charades, and goes on with his breathless conversation.

We walk through the Me'a Shearim neighborhood — through the main street but also into the courtyards and by-ways. This is just exactly like Poland, Chaim explains. Exactly how it was. There is no difference. The people have ten and twelve children and look how they live crowded in one room. They are of the Satmar sect — they also live in Williamsburg in Brooklyn and in Monroe, New York, and do not like the State of Israel. They fight with the Chabadniks, who are Zionists — over this point. They believe that until the Messiah comes the Jews have no business to make a state here. We also walk the outskirts of the religious neighborhood (which, by the way, is quite old, narrow streets, quite picturesque, cobbled) to the pre '67 border area with the then Arab city of Jerusalem where all the buildings bear the marks of that war — bullet holes, broken windows, some of the buildings are even redone in a fortress-like arrangement, their window openings cemented in, leaving only a tiny opening through which a gun can be pointed.

Then we go back into the neighborhood to synagogue. On the way we meet a young dark man looking grim and athletic who Chaim explains is an Israeli war hero, winner of the highest medal for bravery. You would never guess it to look at him, Chaim says. Once when I was walking with him in the border area he picked up a, you know what it is, it is long, and it bites, Eve was tempted by this...a snake? Exactly!—and he picked it up with his bare hands and killed it.

Chaim also explains, in response to my question about how the Satmar sect support themselves, that they are supported by the Jewish Mafia, who they somehow own. And that some Canadian Jew, who he's amazed I haven't heard of, has recently given them one hundred million dollars for their various Yeshivot.

Many people begin gathering in the streets, proceeding on their way to synagogue. They appear as if by magic — a few moments before there was not a soul to be seen anywhere — now, suddenly — one by one— and in bigger and bigger groups— they appear— and now they are a crowd, and in another moment we hear the siren that announces, officially, the arrival of Shabbat. A few people hurry by — then more and more. Many people are dressed in the archaic costumes — payes (forelocks); black hats; some with long grayish coats that look like bathrobes; some wearing eighteenth century hose with knickers; some with the round fur hats.

Chaim takes us to an Ashkenazi synagogue, one of the three or four synagogues which he attends regularly. Apparently here the system is quite different from the States. Rather than have a central synagogue for each neighborhood, here there are synagogues everywhere — it seems in Jerusalem every other building is a synagogue — in fact on our tour, Chaim shows us a synagogue complex — four synagogues right next to one another — but all of them full, overflowing, so we have to go elsewhere — and one simply goes here or there to a synagogue, no need to join or be officially affiliated in any way. The government supports the synagogues financially, so there is no need for dues or fund raising; additional funds come spontaneously from people on a volunteer basis. There are no rabbis as such — in Israel there are so many rabbis that the concept of a rabbi is completely different. rabbis here are doctors, lawyers, scientists, soldiers, clerks, and only a very few of them function as full-time heads of congregations. In most of the synagogues whoever is by custom and mutual assent considered the oldest and the wisest among the many rabbis in the group who regularly pray at that synagogue becomes the leader of that group and delivers the sermon when one is required. Someone else volunteers to be the shamus, taking care of the building, opening it and closing it as necessary, seeing to its upkeep. According to Chaim, the whole system is very informal and simple.

The synagogue itself is quite small and simple — reminds me very much of the simple shuls we saw in Zefat. About the size of a classroom, with a raised pulpit in the middle of the room surrounded by a railing, facing the ark at one end of the room, with a bookcase for prayer books and benches on either side of tables instead of pews. People sit around the benches, some facing the pulpit, others with their backs to it, to pray.

In this neighborhood, Chaim says, it seems every other old man who dies makes it his dying wish that his home should become a synagogue.

There are quite simple decorations — the pillars are painted; the wallpaper is a little bit fancy; some design around the ark itself. Hebrew writing above each window.

This particular synagogue is unusual in that there are various kinds of people praying here, as evidenced by the variety of costumes.

We pray with great dispatch, then have to wait for darkness to descend before we can actually begin the Sabbath prayers (this particular shul is very strict on this point, about which there are various conflicting traditions, and it is because of this strictness that Chaim goes here on Friday nights.)

The rabbi delivers a sermon in Hebrew.

Finally it is dark, we finish the service, and out we go.

People in the streets everywhere pouring out from the various synagogues, we are up above standing on the landing watching the people down below. The Yemenite synagogue is just up the street a few doors and from there come people wearing tallith (prayer shawls) — it is a Yemenite tradition to wear them even on Friday night, the others do not, and among the crowd I notice Chaim's venerable uncle, in his traditional Yemenite costume (colored robe, large colored kipah), a very old man who seems absorbed in the act of walking, and around whom there floats an aura of respect and holiness. Everyone from the various synagogues mingles together, wishing each other happy Shabbat, shaking hands, talking, going back home for the family feast.

Back at Chaim's house in the large dining room with its heavy wooden old world furniture sitting at table which is rapidly filling with artfully arranged platters — peanuts, popcorn, salad, walnuts, fruits. We have agreed for the moment not to discuss our misunderstanding. Chaim's point of view is that certainly, obviously, we must stay for the whole of Shabbat. This means overnight and all day tomorrow. He mentions how marvelous it seemed to his mother that we arrived without bags — how could we Americans who are really so superior yet so baffling manage to stay overnight bringing no luggage not even to all appearances a toothbrush or a change of underwear. (According to Jewish law incidentally it is forbidden to carry on the Sabbath. Only when a kosher line is drawn around an area can carrying be done within that area and in fact such a line has been drawn around Jerusalem.) The Yemenite — or perhaps it is general to Judaism — custom at table is men on one side, women on the other. And so we sit formally, Chaim at table's head, bubbling over with enthusiasm for the Sabbath, our presence, the state of Israel, God.

Drink, drink, he says after kiddush is made. Sit, drink. He pours Scotch for us, and when my father refuses to drink for health reasons — he needs to take pills and is not sure the mixture will not cause fainting — Chaim says it is the Shabbat it is God's day. The rest of the week we do what we need to do but today! We drink to God he says, belting back a glass of Scotch. During the week I never drink only on Shabbat. But all week long I smoke. All week smoking like crazy but on Shabbat — I forget it! Don't even think of it! Then as soon as Shabbat is over I remember the cigarettes, I am looking all over the place, where is the cigarettes, come on Mama! Mama! She says to start without her but I cannot start. She is afraid I am laughing at her. Come and eat.

It takes a long time for Chaim to concede that my father is not going to drink the Scotch.

Come sing, do you know any songs, sing what you know, says Chaim. And we do sing, Hebrew songs from our childhood — Chaim and his wife and his mother also know them — and we all sing quite nicely together until we run out of songs, pretty quickly. It is good to sing songs my father, brother, and I, that we sang many years ago when we were together as a family — if ever we in fact were. Perhaps I am only wishing we were at one time. Perhaps although our family was not a particularly unhappy one, it was not an especially happy one either. There were occasional songs. Outside we hear singing coming from other houses nearby.

It takes also a long time of talking and eating before we get through this course of the meal and onto the next — chicken soup — then the next — three kinds of Yemenite bread — one like a big pancake, one like a floppy pita, one like a cake soaked with chicken grease and embedded with chunks of some kind of chicken organ meat — all very delicious (and they also have a challah for us in case we don't like the traditional bread)—then the next, chicken with rice and baked potato, artfully prepared. It is not easy for us to down all this food but we do it — except for Dad who is quite embarrassed in general at the childlike portions he eats and even more so now.

Chaim does not eat any chicken. His plate includes only potato and rice. Why? Because I am one hundred percent vegetarian, one hundred percent natural. You will see after dinner the tea we have one hundred percent vegetarian. When my mother was in the USA for the engagement party she said that the vegetables and the — mm — how do you say that one — round, sweet, as — exactly! the fruit, was very big and looks very good, but no taste! They make it so big, pick it green. But here — everything tastes so good, so fresh. One hundred percent vegetarian. It says in the Bible, what is it? He quotes a Hebrew phrase — to which Dad responds happily, Land of milk and honey. Exactly! Land of milk and honey. All the things that are grown here you could not believe it! Avocados, mangos, we have bananas, lettuce, potato, wheat, such sweet fruits, prickly pear, just like in the Bible you couldn't believe it how it all grows here everywhere, up in the Galilee — you saw it. The young peoples here, the Ashkenazi, they get so big from eating all this food, but no I think also it is because of the Shoah, how do you say it, Holocaust. Exactly! Just like a plant. They did already a study of this. If you pinch the plant and hurt it badly it will produce really strong seeds. They studied that the victims of the Shoah their children are twice as big as them, twice as big as we Yemenites, though we eat the same food, because of the Shoah. They're big! Strong, you should see what I mean. Why I'm one hundred percent vegetarian? Because of the war, when I was in the army I decided. You've seen one of those — grenades? Exactly! Yes, this is an Israeli one — it's up on the mantle next to the ancient Hebrew prayer books, handwritten, falling apart, that had been in Chaim's family back more generations than he knows about. The grenade has a small sea shell stuck into its mouth. They think only they fought a war, my father says to me in an aside. Next to the grenade is an object that looks like a cross between a billy club and a swagger stick. Chaim unsheathes it — a dagger. I got also in the war, in Lebanon, he says. I wonder if he took it off a PLO guy after he killed him, my father says to me in an aside.

Chaim's mother and wife listen to all this, apparently understanding a little. Both of them lovely in their pure white Shabbat dresses, a little tired, very innocent, a little drunk.

The conversation continues to sail onward, propelled by Chaim's enthusiasm for life in general and the English language in particular.

He is a scribe which means he writes out longhand the Torah scrolls, mezzuzoth, and teffilin scrolls. This is very difficult work. There are so many rules — and one little mistake and you start over again. It takes about a year to write a Torah scroll. Under these circumstances I wonder how anyone can afford to purchase one, but they do. Yemenite Jews came to Israel soon after 1948 in a dramatic mass emigration airlift known as Operation Magic Carpet (they had never seen planes before). For centuries they had lived in Yemen cut off from the Jewish world but maintaining Jewish culture, completely separate from but living in harmony with their Yemenite Arab neighbors. It had always been a dream, a prophecy, that they would one day return to the Holy Land — "on the wings of an eagle"— and when the Operation Magic Carpet planes landed in Israel full of these incredulous backward people the prophecy had surely come true. Chaim explains that here in Israel we are all Israelis, all Jews, and the Yemenites, although their customs differ somewhat do not attempt to preserve the way of life of the Diaspora. He explains that in the old country it was the custom for the women to marry at about age eight, to boys about sixteen or eighteen years old. His mother was married at about that age, and gave birth to her first child at twelve or thirteen. Chaim himself is thirty-two. His wife is eighteen and looks younger.

At eleven o'clock the automatically-timed lights go off and we are in near-darkness only a gas all-night light is left on to dimly illuminate the room. Conversation goes on for a while but the darkness, the meal, and the whiskey, make us all sleepy and we say that we have to begin the walk back to our hotel. Chaim is too tired now to argue with us about staying over and we have been absolutely firm on this point, so he offers to walk part way back with us.

The carless midnight streets are full of Shabbat strollers on their way home after a joyous night of visiting. The streets are absolutely packed with families in their finery — little boys and girls toddling along with their parents, teen-agers dressed in Hasidic costumes in roving jolly bands, men in fur hats and silver robes, people greeting one another, stopping to talk. The night is warm and pleasant and there is a wonderful feeling of calmness and satisfaction afoot, as though tonight has been an absolutely unique and special night in human history and now it was drawing sweetly and perfectly to a close, everyone full of good food and deliciously fatigued from singing drinking laughing and talking.

Next morning we attend Shabbat services at the Great Synagogue of Jerusalem — the official state synagogue. A huge impressive modern building with a large dome over the pulpit and a majestic stained glass window behind the ark, it is surprisingly empty of worshippers — not of course empty, but not nearly as full as we had imagined. Dad was afraid we'd be unable to find a seat, arriving rather late as we did. Instead there are many seats, and the usher leads us to some good ones, right near the front.

The seats are quite marvelous — they are comfortable and flop up as soon as you rise, creating quite a large space to stand in or to move through if you need to come or go. And there are good little lecterns in front of each seat cleverly designed so that you can easily fix your book on them — but when you stand up (up flops your seat) they adjust so that now you can fix your book on them so that it will be convenient from this height too. They were clearly designed by someone who knows the ins and outs of serious prayer, which in Judaism is not entirely a matter of the heart, but is also a technical feat, which must be studied, practiced, prepared for, entered into, refined.

The worshippers represent a variety of types of people — some ultra-orthodox, but in the main modern orthodox types, some in suits, some in shirt sleeves, some younger, but most older. All men of course. The women are upstairs, like a circle of angels surrounding the dome above.

As we arrive the Haftorah is being chanted by an old man. Everyone follows along very carefully, with concentration, and as the man finishes and turns to leave we discover that he is blind, he can barely move, he is congratulated and helped carefully down from the pulpit by several friends, and many people, especially children, surround him to congratulate him, but he seems to be somewhere else, he is neither relieved nor happy, he does not seem to know where he is, he is trying only to keep from falling over, and to get somehow to his seat.

While this is going on the cantor, a large broad slightly portly man wearing black robes and a high black skull cap makes a gesture to his young son, who is running toward him to bring him his prayerbook — sh — don't run — be a good boy — you are in the synagogue. His gesture is so studied yet informal expressing his own confidence as a leader and performer, representative of the people to God, a respected member of the community with a great voice. He seems to enjoy himself very much, to eat very well, to enjoy his work.

He rises to the pulpit to sing and is in total command — his voice with its impressive range and tone scattering all over the room. There is a bit too much drama to the singing, to my taste. There are at least five or six ultimate musical moments in the next half hour or so of musical prayer. Mostly the worshippers listen as the cantor and choir perform. They do respond and sing themselves, but not much and only half-heartedly. This is clearly a professional affair, the best in town. The choir of tallith-clad young men is quite good. But the choral pieces sound a little obvious to me.

At a crucial moment in the service many men clatter up to the front of the synagogue before the ark, face the congregation, and cover their faces with their tallithim. They look like a swaying lunatic gaggle of ghosts. This is the famous blessing of the Cohanim that Dad was telling us about the other day. They used to do it when he was a kid, at the orthodox shul in Exeter, Pennsylvania. The people at the orthodox shul there felt that the Conservative Jews in Pittston (where we grew up) were just like goyim — hardly Jews at all. They didn't do anything the kosher way. Mr. Siegel, the Exeter rabbi, was very kosher. He was from the old country. He spoke only Yiddish. He had no fancy American training, in fact he wasn't a rabbi at all, he was a shoychet, a ritual slaughterer, and I can remember watching him kill chickens by slitting their throats and waving them around for a while until all the blood was let and they stopped jerking. He was very good at it, very definite about it. I also remember him throwing back shots of schnapps at the kiddushim after service on Saturday mornings. The goyim in Pittston did not practice the Cohanim blessing. The blessing went like this: the Cohanim, those few Jews in the congregation that came from family lineages descended from Aaron, the High Priest, in the days of the Temple, stood in front of the congregation, covered their faces up with their tallithim, and, under cover of the tallithim, made secret gestures with their fingers. Dad said that the story was if you looked at them when they did it you'd die. So when they did it everyone in the congregation turned their backs to them, afraid to look.

Here in the Great Synagogue of Jerusalem, however, where there are at least twenty or so Cohanim, a very impressive number, it is OK to watch. They are covered anyway with tallithim and swing back and forth eerily. They make the secret gesture with their fingers pointed toward the congregation, which pushes outward at the tallithim so that they all have weird draped shapes as they sing, repeating in shaky banshee-like disorganized voices the blessing which is sung by the cantor first, line by line, in his striking baritone.

The service concludes with a hymn led by a young boy — not more than five or six, whose strong clear soprano is truly memorable. After the hymn is over he sits on his father's knee while the concluding announcements are made. His father is very proud of him, almost glowing, as is the son, with good feeling.

JAPAN

I'M IN JAPAN, SITTING IN THE MONK'S QUARTERS of Rinso-in
temple in Yaizu, with the sliding paper doors open overlooking
the carp pond that Suzuki-roshi made many years ago. The story
goes that he moved that big boulder into place by himself and that
he broke his finger doing it and his finger after that was crooked.
There is a stained glass window in the Zen Center in San Francisco
that depicts Suzuki-roshi's hands with this crooked finger. The
boulder is covered with moss rich deep and green in the late afternoon light. The carp are red white and tan moving around slowly
in the pond. It's very peaceful very quiet inside this simple bare
tatami mat room, but soon Hojo-san, Suzuki-roshi's son, who is
now abbot of this, his father's temple, calls me into the Hondo:
it's time to start getting ready for tonight's samisen and story-
telling performance. Hustle bustle, lots to do, vacuum, dust,
straighten up, the place is a mess, set up the screens, check out the
lighting, move things around. I am running around doing all this.
A lot of members of the congregation are there helping, lots of
little dark agile people jabbering away at each other loudly in
Japanese. Chitosae, Hojo-san's wife is there, Hojo-san himself,
various other helpers are telling me do this, do that, move this
here, go get that, but they are telling me all of this in Japanese and

they are very excited and I don't speak a single word of Japanese. I've even forgotten how to say "I'm sorry, I don't speak Japanese." One of the light fixtures has burned out and they send me here or there to get another but I don't know what's going on. I am twice as big as anyone else in the room and I feel twice as stupid and four times as clumsy. I haven't been feeling well all day and all of this running around and confusion and especially all of the Japanese language flying around the room which always seems dramatic, like in the Toshiro Mifune movies, where no one just talks, they emote, is really getting me sicker by the minute, and they hand me the fluorescent light bulb and motion me go ahead screw it in there's no ladder or chair to stand on I suppose they think that because I am so tall I can easily change a light bulb that is ten feet from the floor.

I stand there like an idiot with Japanese words clanking around in my head and banging up against the sides of my head and with my stomach churning and seeing that I can't do this simple thing like change a light bulb (because I don't know how to say "I need a chair or something where's a chair or something to stand on?") somebody else grabs the light bulb and gets a ladder and changes the bulb while I stand there huge as a person can be in the middle of the room while everyone runs around me doing this and that. Then they hustle me off to the zendo where we have to move some heavy platforms and bring them into the Hondo to set up a stage for the samisen player and storyteller. The platform is really heavy and everything is happening very fast, the other men are very quick and they can talk to one another about how to lift it and they tell me how to grab it this way that way shift it this way that way but I can't understand a word they're saying and they say it again, louder, but never stop moving, we're in a hurry, the performance is in less than an hour and really it is very hard for them to understand how such a really very large person can't understand these simple things they are saying.

That night I am sick during the performance and in my semi - conscious delirium I can hear the samisen music and the dramatic words of the storyteller and it all makes me more and more sick.

Actually, although I feel pretty out of place here, as though everyone but me shared a wonderful secret, I like it pretty well in Japan. There is a wonderful smoothness and politeness to the way people are, a grace and skill in living, a balance and contentment, that everyone seems to exhude. The Japanese seem to understand each other intuitively, and they seem to belong very much to the places they inhabit, to feel comfortable with themselves and their lives. When we go with Hojo-san to the noodle shop with all his friends, everyone talks easily together and seems to enjoy the noodles, the company, and the day. The streets of Yaizu are very narrow, often only wide enough for a single car to pass, and with no sidewalks, so the pedestrians also walk on the street, and yet there are no problems with this. People just back up for one another in their cars. No one seems to get rattled.

The word "Japan" means "the place where the sun comes up." The word "Israel" means "contention." From the very beginning the Jews struggled with God; God chose them but they did not necessarily want to be chosen. They were promised the land, probably a kind of bribe, and they went toward the land, but were immediately caused to wander around in the worst and most confusing way, had to fight their way in, and were later defeated and exiled, kicking and screaming and fighting amongst themselves the whole while. Far from working out carefully how to live where they were, they were engaged in a continual struggle to establish their right to be there. Since the beginning nothing ever worked out quite right and so it was quite clear that this world was not workable and since God would not have made a world like this for nothing surely there was going to be a better world later on, a millennium, the age of the Messiah. Jews have always been Utopians. Karl Marx is the greatest Jewish Utopian after Moses and Jesus. He crossed out the word "God" and substituted the word "history" and he crossed out "the Jew" and substituted "the proletariat." And he cursed and complained and screamed like any Biblical prophet. Things were going to be different, things were going to change, people were going to be different from what they had ever been, he said.

Nothing could be further from the Japanese mind than Utopia. The concept doesn't make sense. This world is Utopia, as far as the Japanese are concerned, and when you see them gathered, as they are at Rinso-in, around the table, happily eating rice and drinking tea, or see them as we did yesterday in the Indigo shop, sewing carefully on beautiful thick wonderful fabric dyed by hand, you know that this is true. There really is an innocence to the Japanese approach to life. They just don't understand how compelling evil can be and so they love the world as it is, they don't need to change it.

I think this must be because of the tea plants and the rice plants. Japanese culture is unimaginable without tea plants and rice plants, and you see these here and there around Yaizu, neatly pruned uniform tea plantations up on the mountain, and beautiful greenish yellow this time of year rice fields pleasing to the eye, stretching on beyond the houses and under the mountain. And always there are people moving in the rice fields and tea plantations, people working with the plants carefully, looking as if they themselves belong to the earth and the fields, as if somehow human life did make sense, was good, could be happy.

The next day we were again in the throes of another special preparation: this time for the annual Founder's Day ceremony at Rinso-in. More sweeping, cleaning, changing flowers on the altar, arranging, fixing, dusting, raking. All the priests from Rinso-in's many subtemples came early and were hanging around while Hojo-san held a lengthy rehearsal with his choir of elderly women, all dressed in black robes, each with a handbell and a gong. There was some beautiful singing and then the ringing of the bells and the striking of the gongs, all fifty or so of them in unison. Over and over again Hojo-san rehearsed the simple tunes, belting them out at the top of his lungs lustily, his voice straining as he urged them on to higher and higher levels of musical transcendence.

The Hondo looked beautiful for the ceremony, the high dark wood altar full of food offerings and flowers, red, white, blue, green and yellow banners hanging from the ceiling, gold lacquered rings and ornaments hanging also from the ceiling. The old men sitting on low tables smoking and laughing off to one side. The old women looking very serious and concentrated in the middle of the Hondo, bells and gongs in hand, and all us Zen priests in our full regalia, black robes, golden-brown okesas (outer ceremonial robes), white tabi (a kind of ceremonial sock), lined up with great decorum. The little old priests from the sub-temples, some of them really tiny round and brown, like little walnuts, standing so quietly. And in the back row we five big American priests, taking our places along with the rest.

The ceremony took a while. There was the sweet singing of the old women. There was a very formal incense offering by all the priests. Many many additional food offerings and full prostrations by Hojo-san. A big formal statement by Hojo-san, and the solemn chanting of a proclamation for the occasion. Then we all bowed and chanted texts in Japanese as we marched around the room in serpentine fashion, in, out, around, and in. After the ceremony all us priests lined up in two long rows on either side of the long narrow reception room, and we had a great feast with beer, sake, and special Chinese plum wine.

We do have some big ceremonies at the Zen Centers in America, but mostly our practice is about meditation and self transformation. In Japan the practice is embedded in, is almost the definition of, the culture. It's like breathing and eating and calligraphy and tea ceremony: things everyone knows about. In America it's the opposite: a way to go beyond your culture, to find a free way outside it.

The next day we were in Tokyo, in a windowless conference room in the Grand Hotel, talking to some officials of the international division of the Soto Zen Headquarters. For a long time we at Zen Center have had very little to do with the Soto Zen Headquarters. But now the Soto Zen Headquarters seems interested to get to know us. Although the young men we were speaking with seemed very earnest and sincere, the conversation was a little hard to follow and a little bureaucratic, so I excused myself and went down to the lobby to poke around. At the front desk I ran into a Japanese priest who had just returned from a visit to America. He spoke a little bit of English. He was pretty agitated when he saw me. There has just been an earthquake, he told me, a terrible earthquake in San Francisco. It's the worst disaster. The bridge fell down. Many buildings fell down. There is a big fire. I ran upstairs to the conference room and told the others and we broke off the meeting right away and went to a television set. It was a very strange feeling to be in the Grand Hotel in Tokyo watching San Francisco burning.

MY MOTHER

At first it was a shock to see her. She didn't look the same at all. Her face was ashen and all puffed up from the chemotherapy and radiation, her arms were huge from it, her hair was matted scarce and a different color, her voice had gone all croaky and harsh, and the medication had got her mixed up and disconnected. She'd sit up in bed all of a sudden, beside herself with anger or frustration, and yell to my Aunt Adeline, No, turn me over, not that way this way, no not that way I said like this like that, and my poor Aunt Adeline would try to be helpful but nothing was helpful. Adeline and my father and my Aunt Sylvia all looked at one another and at me. Their look expressed an unspecified and very confused dismay.

She'd go in and out of consciousness. She'd see things. She said, Don't let them make you do anything you don't want to.

She said, You all think I'm crazy but I know what I'm doing.

She said, Throw away all the envelopes that you can.

She said, Why are you all standing around here. It's ridiculous! Scram!

And she said to me, You're a cute boy in that shirt.

After a while it was very beautiful to see her so earnestly living this simple intense painful but somehow noble existence in the six

178

foot by three foot space of hospital bed that was her whole life. There and the unknown realms of space and time through which she traveled.

She said, Put my shoes in boxes over there.

We'd take shifts staying with her around the clock and I would look forward very much to being with her, to be able to be as intimate with her as I had been as a child and to have a clearer and purer relationship to her than I had been able to have for many many years. She had been for a long time disappointed in my life. She loved me very much and I think felt frustrated in something in her life and so needed me to afford her satisfaction in some way. But I never did that. I had an unusual kind of life. It was very hard for her. But now I could stroke her forehead and try to release the tension I could see building up around her eyes. And I could breathe with her and my doing that would calm her down a little bit. Sometimes if she were making noise in her breathing I'd make noise in the same way. But I couldn't do that when the others were around because it would make them nervous, as though I were doing some kind of voodoo. Sometimes she'd sit up suddenly out of her unconsciousness and say to me, Don't make fun of me. And I'd say I'm not making fun of you. I love you. And late at night I could look at her in the lamp-light and could think of how many ways I could have been nicer to her and how much she'd loved me and given to me and I could tell her how much I loved her and it would make me cry gently. And when she'd suddenly sit up and say, My hat, or, Get my shoes, we're going out, or Where are the red and green charts they should be up by now. I'd tell her, Don't worry about that. Your life is very simple now. Just breathe. And she'd lie back down and feel calmer and reassured.

Gradually during the days and nights she began to give everything up. First her body became more relaxed, as though it weren't hers anymore. Then she stopped having any sense of whether she liked or didn't like anything. Then she couldn't tell who anyone was or what anything was in the room. Then all of the worries and cares of her life began swimming around in her delirium, her clothes, things she had to do at home or for my father, things at the office where she worked, and one by one she put them down too. Finally there was only a dim awareness that got finer and finer as her breath seemed to go more and more deep more and more inward. The heavy earth of her body dissolved into water. The water of the moving of her blood dissolved into the fire of the images that receded in the distance. The fiery images dissolved into air and the air into space, endless space and endless consciousness.

My father cried and said It isn't fair, as my sons arguing with one another or carefully watching each other divide some special food often say. It isn't fair.

I knew she was gone but it didn't really make sense that she was gone. Because she didn't go anywhere. And the gone that she was was really no different from the gone that she had usually been to me my whole adult life and even, a little bit more and more each day, in my life as a child. In one way she was gone. But in another way she was very present. We stood there looking at her. She looked very noble and we were all in awe of her. Then everyone wanted to leave and I said, Is it all right if I stay with her a while and everyone said yes it was all right and they left.

It was nearly dawn. The light coming in the window was lovely and my mother looked lovely in the light. Her skin was a different color than it had ever been before. It looked very very soft and gentle. I could see that she had many freckles on her face. I had never noticed before that she had freckles. I felt like talking to her. I said, Don't be confused!

Then I quietly recited the Heart Sutra. It says, Form is emptiness, emptiness is form, everything that is form is emptiness, everything that is emptiness form. And it says, There are no eyes no ears no nose no tongue no body and no mind. There is no color no sound no smell no taste no touch no mental object. And it says, There is nothing to have and the mind is no hindrance. And it ends, Gone, gone, gone, completely gone, gone beyond everything. I have recited this sutra thousands of times but I never felt so clearly as now what it meant.

I looked out the window. The Florida hospital lawns were pale green in the dawn light, very quiet and pure, as if brand new, with no one around. My mother was all right. She had everything she needed. Far away on the lawn a workman appeared and tried to start a lawnmower. It took many many pulls before he got it going. And then silently and slowly he began pushing it back and forth across the lawn. Mama was all right. But it was going to be hard for the world with all its struggle and fragility and beauty to get along without her and then I cried a lot for the world that didn't know any peace and perhaps never would.

TO MY MOTHER LENORA FISCHER (1922–1985)

Like no other time before now or afterward
What I feel for you dissolves my limbs
As if the edges of my body were a lie I was caught in
Or an excuse that only a lie could resolve
I want to break out of this to get to your side
Because the totality of the peace you bring
Puts this world with its trees rumors and meals to shame
And although we never understood each other in ordinary ways
We cannot choose either more or less what we'll be influenced by
The moon is bright tonight just rising over the top of the peak
What tracks will the moon's path leave what marks in the sky?
I will go there. I will embark on this story.
What would these enigmatic poems mean
Once they tore themselves from me against my will
And who would claim credit for them?
Would a kind of future life be assured or is the sky
Enough this warm summer's night whose problem
Does not seem a problem from your side
Time's slide greased by thought our love
Born of a closeness neither one of us could bear
I think we had the fault of excessive hope

And were disappointed with time expecting fullness
To be an augmentation of the present more than it would hold
Hours and minutes add up to an inspiration we did not see
And could not endure where you are in wholeness
Time comes to you in floating chunks now and I can see
You mixed in with what's between the places of my life
Eleven months have passed since I began this dialog with you
Each sentence longing for the entire poem

KING DAVID'S TOMB

In 1000 B.C. DAVID, POET AND WARRIOR, conquered the city of Jerusalem, taking it over from the Jebusites, establishing once and for all the Kingdom of Israel with Jerusalem as its symbolic head.

David wrote, I do believe I shall yet see the goodness of the Lord in the land of the living.

As was the custom he razed to the ground the previous city, killed the inhabitants, and built his city on the rubble.

I wonder if he imagined that the same thing would not happen again to his city, that eternally it would stand. Or did he think that of course it too would be destroyed and buried at some later time, and that he was one among many actors in a chain of occurrences that would continue endlessly. Or were perhaps such thoughts one way or another alien altogether to his mind. He seems to have had a very close relationship to God. Perhaps he was in constant communication with God and so did not consider his acts at all from the standpoint of time but only as final absolute acts. I think it must be possible to find the answers to these questions by reading David's Psalms and the Bible deeply. Perhaps if I found out the answers to these questions I could begin to understand a little bit about the politics, if they really are politics, of this place.

What remains of David's city is a modest series of stone ruins running up the steep hillside that is southeast of the Old City of Jerusalem. Terraced steps and walkways take you on a walking tour of the site, complete with small maps with explanations mounted on metal posts. But though we read the maps and look at the stones, we cannot visualize the geography of the city. Nevertheless here, as elsewhere in Israel, the stones themselves, the sun beating on them, suggest and evoke an ancient presence.

Behind us, across the Kidron valley, is the Arab town of Silwan. It looks as if it has not changed for hundreds of years, ramshackle huts built one next to another, apparently newer ones on top of ruined ones, somehow caves are built right into the structure of the village.

Below the village, running along the bottom of the valley and beyond, extending up the hillside to the west, is the ancient Jewish burial ground. The hillside is covered with graves. Below are a few tombs for the ancient kings of Israel. This is a very special burial ground for it is, according to tradition, the first place where the dead will be raised up after the Judgment Day.

I wonder whether people of ancient times really believed this. Did they actually think that the condition of death was a temporary one? If they did they were very different from us. Once, many years ago, I spent a good deal of time with members of the Jehovah's Witnesses because they espouse the doctrine that they will, literally, not die, because the Judgment Day will be coming in their very lifetimes. I hung around with them because I wanted to find out what life would be like if you really thought you weren't going to die. But I never did find out and I ended up doubting whether they really did believe this. I think they wanted to believe it but I do not think they actually did.

We walk again up and around the Old City walls and veer off to visit the Garden of Gethsemane. A large church stands here, very busy, many pilgrims, and an Arab man with a camel you can climb on and have your picture taken with. The camel is kneeling down in position for people to mount him. I am very impressed with the camel's knees, which allow the legs to fold completely in half. The knees are very horny from contact with the hard street. The camel seems on the whole very composed.

The garden, preserved beside the impressive church, is very small, possesses rows of very ancient olive trees. There is an intensity to it produced by the hot sun, the hard soil, the furious-looking trees that are gnarled and washed-out but not very tall.

Inside, the church is cool and peaceful. It features a huge stained glass window behind the altar depicting Jesus' trials in the garden. Like the camel, he kneels beside a large rock located in a space that seems like nowhere. I think in this church there is also a rock of some sort that comes up near the altar from the bedrock on the ground and must be the rock where Jesus kneeled at that time. The restored mosaic floors have a lot of white in them. The design is clear and beautiful. We sit quietly for a while resting.

Today, in California, I spoke with a Dominican nun about the Holy Land. She told me that if she ever went there she would not go to any of the shrines. She would go to the places where Jesus walked, the countryside. She would take pictures of this countryside.

Jeff and I are looking for David's tomb. Of course this tomb is probably not really David's tomb. But everyone believes it is David's tomb and that's what counts. We wander around in vaulted corridors that sometimes lead to synagogues which are quiet this Shabbat afternoon. We are in some sort of seminary, this one in particular probably for Americans judging by the predominance of English notices on the bulletin boards. No one much around. A few young boys with kipot and forelocks come hooting down the corridors, a family comes by, but otherwise no one. Finally we come to what must be the supposed tomb of David. It is a large rounded plaster unit, like the other tombs we've seen, this one covered with a regal blue velvet cloth, embroidered with stars of David. There are crowns lined up on top of it. It, typical of Jewish monuments we've seen, is not terribly adorned nor impressive nor holy-looking.

We stand in front of the tomb quietly for a long time. This is our last day in Israel. Tomorrow we will fly home and neither of us will ever come to Jerusalem again. I am thinking of my mother, how she looked when she died, and I am thinking of King David, of his passionate love for God, of his total dedication to God, David who wrote, "Day after day pours forth speech and night after night reveals knowledge. There is no speech, there are no words; unheard is their voice. Yet their message extends through all the earth, and their words reach the end of the world."

Standing there in front of David's Tomb (and it is , I now see, David's Tomb) I can hear these unheard words, and I can feel my mother's presence.

We head back into the Old City through St. Stephen's Gate — our last chance to walk the streets and incidentally to pick up a few gifts for friends. Buying gifts is the most difficult part of traveling, I think. You need first to make a list of who you want to buy gifts for, what you think they would like to have, how much you can spend for each gift, how much it comes to total, and then to consider whether these gifts will fit in your suitcase, whether they will break or melt or unravel en route. I find it very difficult to find a suitable gift.

We kneel to look at some interesting painted tiles displayed outside an Arab shop. Jeff notices the tiles are made in Italy and we laugh at the hucksterism of the Arab merchants — but as we are talking the shop owner, a woman of about forty, who has been listening to us, says, no, really, the tiles are from Italy because we have found they make the best tiles, but the painting is done here, by hand, you should come in and look.

We go inside the shop, and look at the woman's paints and brushes, her work in progress. A very large and beautiful selection of tiles in traditional designs is displayed everywhere. We are impressed with their skill and subtlety and begin to pick out many tiles to bring as gifts. As we do so the woman resumes her work. She is a plump very relaxed person who speaks fluent English. She seems quite possessed of herself and paints very fluidly in an easy manner. Her work space is very neatly organized. Her brother works with her in the shop. He seems a bit more nervous. As we are looking at tiles, the brother's children come into the shop. They annoy the brother a little, but the woman receives them calmly as she paints and talks to them quietly and they finally sit and watch her work. It is good work, the woman says, because it is so quiet. It is not a lot of money but after all it is not money so much that matters. I would like to teach the children a little, but how to do it, you don't know if they will want to do it. Now it is Ramadan and there is a month of no school so perhaps I can show them a little something. Would you like to have some tea? Sit. Have some tea. This is our custom.

We sit and one of the children, a young girl of about eleven, pours tea from the samovar. I thank her and tell her, on the first sip, what good tea this is, strong mint tea with honey. It embarrasses her. We drink our tea in silence.

You look like brothers she says, looking us over. People often tell us we look alike but we are not twins, I say.

Later we stop at more Arab shops — I buy a sterling silver necklace with a "stone" fashioned from Roman glass, and even get an official paper, filled out on the spot by the merchant, a boy of about fourteen, that attests that this is in fact genuine Roman glass. I am fascinated with the notion of this glass, collected on archeological digs by the bucketful, that was used in Roman times. The boy tells us that at one time this glass was very plentiful and cheap, but that now the price is going up constantly. Although it sounds exotic, even now such glass is not rare.

Later on Jeff stops to buy a cotton shirt from another merchant. He gets it for something like half what the man originally asks. The first price was, of course, outrageous.

That night we walk down Ben Yehuda Street to have our last look at Jerusalem. Dad, after his long afternoon nap, is excited and talkative. He has been ready to go home for at least a week and now is giddy with anticipation.

Ben Yehuda Street is in the main commercial section of the new Jerusalem. The newly cobbled streets blocked off to automobile traffic, there is a carnival atmosphere here. The streets are jammed with people and lined with sidewalk cafes this warm night. All the eating places are extremely up to date, sophisticated, and the teenagers that frequent them are dressed in the latest international fashions. We sit at the sidewalk table of one of the delis. The food is not terribly good. Israel is infamous for its inferior deli food. Why no one has figured out how to do an authentic New York deli that can cater to the American tourists and therefore will make a million dollars I'll never know. We watch the people swarming on the streets and around our table, families, young couples, but predominantly teenagers out for a date on Saturday night. It is very strange to watch them in their oversized bright colored T-shirts, white high topped sneakers, and acid washed jeans. They remind me of my own children — so tentative, so self-conscious. Probably within a year most of them will be in the army and perhaps some of them will have their names published in the newspaper for throwing some Palestinian children about their own age or even younger off a roof, or for being killed in some local ambush. But perhaps not. Perhaps Moishe and Panina's children and the thousands of children like them raised on the West bank and elsewhere in Israel will become finally tired of fighting endlessly in wars for ideas of land or security or revenge that do not hold any bright place in their minds. Perhaps they will care as much about the fate of this small country as their parents and grandparents did — or even as much as I do — or perhaps they will not. But they will be asked to work out the details. They may not want to do it. They will be told that God demands it of them. I wonder if their refusal, for I think they will refuse to accept the responsibility on terms they themselves have neither created nor even participated in, will be a more or less noble thing than the trials and struggles endured by their forebears for generations.

We pay our bill and leave, and as we are walking up the street I recognize David White, the rabbi from Tiburon, near Green

Gulch. Hey David! He looks at me in amazement. He doesn't know what to say. I am the last person in the world he expected to see here, in Jerusalem. What a coincidence!